Using cognitive methods in the classroom

Teachers have many common needs. Most work in a situation of high demands and expectations, but against a background that reflects a reduced valuation of teachers' efforts. This book is a response to the growing concerns that teachers express about how to deal with a changing politico-educational environment, while providing the best learning experiences for students with diverse skills and abilities in the most effective and fulfilling way.

The authors have worked for the past ten years on building a coherent cognitive education programme which draws on the literatures of educational psychology and educational theory and practice. This book presents the conceptual foundation of their new teaching–learning approach, Process-Based Instruction, and describes the process of introducing new strategies into the context in which a teacher is working. The authors show that PBI can work both as a curriculum model and as a teaching–learning method. As a curriculum model, PBI provides a framework for structuring classroom activities that facilitates effective communication and support for all students. As a teaching–learning method, PBI includes a number of strategies that focus on teaching students how to learn and solve problems.

The book is supported throughout with examples and illustrations of PBI at work. It is primarily aimed at the class teacher, but others involved in education – counsellors, school psychologists, administrators, curriculum developers, lecturers and students – will also find much of interest here.

Adrian Ashman teaches at the Fred and Eleanor Schonell Special Education Research Centre at the University of Queensland. **Robert Conway** teaches at the Special Education Centre at the University of Newcastle, New South Wales.

Using cognitive methods in the classroom

Adrian F. Ashman
and
Robert N.F. Conway

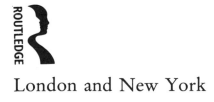

London and New York

First published 1993
by Routledge
11 New Fetter Lane, London EC4P 4EE

Simultaneously published in the USA and Canada
by Routledge
a division of Routledge, Chapman and Hall, Inc.
29 West 35th Street, New York, NY 10001

© 1993 Adrian F. Ashman and Robert N.F. Conway

Typeset in 10/12pt Garamond Original by
J&L Composition Ltd, Filey, North Yorkshire
Printed and bound in Great Britain by
Biddles Ltd, Guildford and King's Lynn

British Library Cataloguing in Publication Data
A catalogue reference for this book is available from the British Library.
ISBN 0-415-06835-5
    0-415-06836-3 (pbk)

Library of Congress Cataloging in Publication Data
has been applied for.

Contents

Figures

Tables

Boxes

Preface

Some time ago we talked to a mutual friend who is a secondary school English teacher. She has been teaching for nearly ten years and, in our estimation, is enthusiastic, committed to her students and profession, and always keen to learn of new ideas and teaching methods.

On that occasion, as had happened in the past, she expressed concern at the pressures and interruptions that were becoming a regular part of her school day. The list was a familiar one to us and to many teachers. There were demands associated with implementing an ever increasing number of curriculum documents, meeting the needs of the wide variety of student abilities in her classes, and assuming increasing administrative responsibilities. In addition, there were numerous other matters that increased her workload. She felt ill-prepared to work with students of very low ability and who lack motivation, and equally unqualified to implement new strategies for gifted students that the regional curriculum specialist was promoting. In addition, the visiting Support (Resource) Teacher was keen to assist one of her students with a learning disability, and the school principal was encouraging her to undertake further university study.

Just to keep up with the weekly schedule meant many hours of lesson preparation and marking, which began late at night when her own family had gone to bed. Her willingness to donate this extra time was declining.

Our friend's circumstances are similar to those of many other primary and secondary teachers in Australia and overseas to whom we have spoken. Many have expressed the same apprehension at the growing number of factors that make the job of teaching children an extremely demanding one.

Teachers have many common needs. Most work in a situation of high demands and expectations, but against a background that reflects a reduced valuation of teachers' efforts. It seems timely to respond to the growing concerns that teachers express about how one can deal with a changing politico-educational environment, while providing the best learning experiences for students with diverse skills and abilities in the most effective and fulfilling way.

There are many answers to these very difficult questions – almost as many as there are educators willing to respond to them. In addition, there is a plethora of new ideas and initiatives being espoused by researchers and educators that compete for the attention of classroom and resource personnel. In this book we share with readers our thoughts about contemporary teaching practice, and suggest an instructional approach that has already been adopted by educators, in several countries including our own.

Over ten years ago, we began building the conceptual foundation of what has now developed into a coherent cognitive education programme – one that draws on the literatures of educational psychology and educational theory and practice. We have entitled this teaching–learning approach Process-Based Instruction (or PBI). We have been sensitive to the demands being placed on teachers – such as our friend to whom we have referred above – at both the primary and secondary levels. We have, therefore, devoted considerable attention to the application of our approach so that it does not place further demands on the teacher's time or resources. For those who have read our earlier book, *Cognitive strategies in special education* (Routledge, 1989), this book provides an updated model and a more detailed description of the implementation of PBI in a greater range of educational contexts than were presented in the 1989 book.

The purpose of this book is threefold. First, we wish to present the conceptual foundation of PBI, recognizing that it is as important to understand why as it is to understand how. Second, we wish to describe the process of introducing PBI into the context in which a teacher is working. Third, we wish to indicate how teachers and other school personnel may work together to refine and extend PBI within their school or education system. It stands to reason, then, that teachers are the primary audience for this book. Others involved in education – counsellors, school psychologists, school administrators, curriculum developers, university academics and students – will also find much of interest in this volume. There may also be many parents who have an education background who may find PBI of interest as a framework for home-based learning experiences.

While we have chosen not to divide the book into discrete sections, the chapter titles reflect three groups. Chapters 1 to 3 provide the conceptual basis of Process-Based Instruction. Chapters 4 to 8 detail the methods and procedures involved. Chapters 9 and 10 deal with support networks and ways of overcoming problems met by teachers once they have put PBI into practice.

We urge readers to work through the chapters in the order in which they have been presented, thereby building the framework and the practical skills in a systematic way. Some teachers may decide to go directly to Chapter 4 and move on from there. If you do, we encourage you to return to the first three chapters to fill in the theoretical background as soon as you can.

Numerous people have assisted us during the preparation of this book. Many teachers have provided comments and critiques of PBI as they have been using it in their own teaching practice. Such responses have enabled us to refine PBI classroom practices and the in-service programme. In some cases, comments have also led us to reconsider the application of some basic PBI ideas. In particular, we are very appreciative of our colleagues who have given us comments on the various versions of the book as we have been writing. To Patrick Garrahy, Patricia Hunt, Lyndall Hopton, Sharon Ladkin and Susan Wright we offer our most sincere thanks.

Chapter 1

Emerging educational technologies

The developers of any new educational technology must be aware of the environment into which it is to be introduced and the interactions that take place within it. Such interactions will involve the curriculum, teaching practices, the teaching profession, and system and administrative requirements that generally apply. Process-Based Instruction (PBI) was developed after consideration was given to the contribution of each of these four influences, taken separately and together. It is both a curriculum model and a teaching–learning method. As a curriculum model, PBI provides a framework for structuring classroom activities that facilitates effective communication and support for all students. As a teaching–learning method, PBI includes a number of strategies that focus on teaching students how to learn and solve problems.

In this chapter we will:

- identify some of the pressures being experienced by teachers in the current education climate;
- outline some of the basic premises of PBI; and
- describe how PBI can be of value to teachers and students in most educational settings.

New teaching and learning programmes and packages – often called educational technologies – are constantly being introduced to teachers and school personnel. Many are short-lived, being assigned a relatively low priority when compared with other factors that influence the teacher's professional life. These include:

- the effect of incorporating new curriculum policies and guidelines into classroom teaching practices;
- the challenge of planning and presenting appropriate learning experiences for children with mixed abilities and ages in the same class;
- the problems of determining appropriate classroom organization and student management procedures;
- changes in the professional status of teaching and the influence of direct government intervention in educational practices;

- the need to resolve any apparent contradiction between the ideals and teaching methods presented during pre-service training and the practical realities of classroom practice;
- changes to the ongoing (in-service) training of teachers and the need to update their teaching skills;
- changes in the level of teacher accountability, particularly as they affect promotion opportunities;
- the reorganization of educational systems to make school administrators more accountable for their financial and educational decisions;
- the difficulties involved in demonstrating the long-term educational values of new technologies; and
- the need to address all of the above issues within the time constraints of the professional day (and night).

The interaction among the ten factors listed above regulate the introduction of new educational technologies. Those who seek to change existing classroom practices must, therefore, take into account the teachers' needs and those of other school personnel. Figure 1.1 represents our perception of the educational environment into which any new technology must fit. The most crucial interactions are those between the curriculum, teaching practice, and the teaching profession.

THE CURRICULUM AND TEACHING PRACTICE

The curriculum may be developed at the national level (as in the United Kingdom[1]), at the state level (as in Australia), at the school district level or even the local school level. Curriculum documents developed at any of these levels frequently dictate not only the content to be taught, but also the teaching and learning strategies that teachers are to employ. Therefore, any new technology must be evaluated in the light of the time available for teachers to adapt their current procedures or strategies and to implement changes that are consistent with the requirements of the curriculum. The schema in Figure 1.1 represents a common situation in which curriculum policy is developed at a national or state level. Hence, teacher needs are influenced directly by content-driven curricula (e.g., syllabi) and relevant instructional strategies, and the associated priorities and demands imposed by them.

Implementing the curriculum requires teachers and other school or system personnel to make judgements about how it can be taught and learned. New initiatives and technologies are evaluated in relation to current teaching practices and the underlying philosophies held at the time.

While there is an implicit (and sometimes explicit) demand on teachers to keep abreast of current trends and the latest terminology, they are understandably often reluctant to implement new programmes that involve extended preparation or work, along with their existing teaching loads. New approaches that are expressed in jargon terms, or which appear unduly abstract, are unlikely to be accepted, even though they may contain more

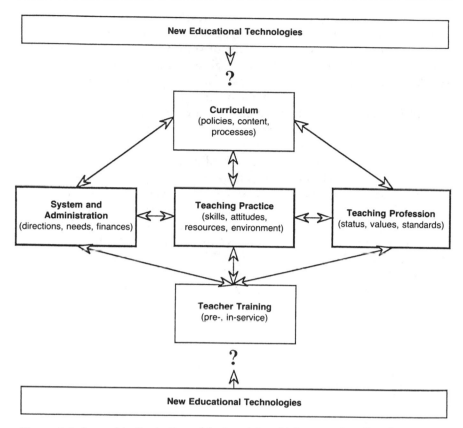

Figure 1.1 A graphic illustration of factors into which new educational technologies must fit

effective teaching and/or learning strategies than are in common use. It is incumbent upon advocates of innovative technologies to demonstrate clearly improved educational outcomes without additional educational 'costs' (e.g., preparation and teaching time or costly resource outlays).

When teachers are convinced that new teaching or learning programmes (new technologies) will work for them, the initial response can be solely at the level of the individual classroom. In other situations, a technology may be introduced as a whole-school professional development initiative. Rarely would (or should) a successful new technology commence at the educational systems level, because the overwhelming majority of teachers would not have had the opportunity to participate in its development and trialing. The antagonisms of teachers toward imposed new technologies mirror those expressed toward imposed curriculum strategies and content.

If curriculum content is prescribed – as in many school systems – one of the most commonly expressed concerns of teachers is its application within mixed ability or composite classes. Many teachers find that the amount of content to be covered in a lesson (term, semester or year) prevents them being able to meet the needs of groups of students within their classes, let alone the needs of individuals. Having a gifted student within the same class as others who are considered to be slow learners creates a situation which many teachers may find to be beyond their personal programming skills. It is difficult within secondary schools, for example, to prepare lessons for a number of classes across grades, without the additional 'burden' of multiple lessons within those classes.

The difficulties encountered in mixed-ability classrooms are closely related to matters of classroom organization and control. When teachers are unable (or perhaps unwilling) to meet students' diverse learning needs, they increase the risk of control problems that result when a class group reflects a broad range of student characteristics – from those who are unable to cope with the learning task (slow learners) to those already able to do the task unassisted (above-average ability). Teachers of mixed-ability classes occasionally express concern about ceding some control over the learning process to students, even though they are unable to teach all students at the one time. Some teachers find that releasing control to students is threatening. Mixed-ability teaching may require the teacher to learn new organizational skills, including group work, student self-regulation and classroom management. However, the acquisition of these skills is often independent of the evaluation and perhaps adoption of new technologies, as they are skills that all teachers should possess.

THE TEACHING PROFESSION AND TEACHING PRACTICE

The teaching profession has always been subject to close scrutiny. There is a perception by some teachers (and unions) that the education system has been subject to greater government intervention in recent years, which has led to a marked decline in teacher morale. Certainly some government interventions have clearly been designed to promote a political agenda; the reader will, no doubt, be able to cite local examples. In other cases, curriculum change has resulted from pressure groups forcing change in educational practices that suit the needs of that group. In both cases the classroom teacher may not support the changes and be reluctant to implement policy, content and strategies in whose development they have played no part.

Moves in a number of countries toward national curricula contrast with moves toward school-based curriculum development. Moves toward an immersion approach to reading as part of a total approach to language development contrast with a skills-based approach to reading and spelling.

Low morale within differing sections of the teaching profession results from a lack of awareness of the efforts made by teachers to adapt to ever-changing and increasing demands on educational systems. While we support the principle of integrating students with special needs into regular classes, the practicalities associated with this policy has left many teachers ill-prepared in terms of their knowledge of appropriate instructional strategies. The lack of training at the pre- and in-service levels has meant that many teachers have been left to implement new curricula and integration strategies unsupported. One can only ask: 'Who is responsible?'

The issue of training raises two additional concerns in the profession: the dichotomy between what is taught during teacher training and how teaching occurs in the classroom, and the reduced availability of in-service training as part of the teaching day. Many students leave teacher training institutions with a general understanding of curriculum requirements and with a broad view of educational practices and strategies. They are often confronted, however, with an in-school belief that 'what you learned in the ivory tower will not work in the real world'! Beginning teachers quickly learn the value of accommodating to the current school or staff room philosophy of educational practice, but the division between the ideals instilled in them during training and the ideals expressed by experienced colleagues can be a source of internal conflict.

It has long been incumbent upon the community to provide a suitable education for all children. In some countries, such as the United States and the United Kingdom, politicians have affirmed this community responsibility through the passage of laws such as PL 94–192 and the Education Act respectively. In countries in which the provision of the most appropriate education is more a professional obligation than a legal requirement (e.g., Australia) there are, nevertheless, powerful bureaucratic pressures imposed on teachers to accept responsibility for the quality of education.

For decades, education systems have assumed responsibility for innovation in teaching practice. Educational administrators – many themselves teachers by profession – have seen value in providing extensive in-service programmes on many contemporary issues such as curriculum initiatives, policies and practices. Such courses, however, have tended to attract conscientious teachers, rather than those for whom the content is more vital. Moves by some educational authorities in recent years to link pay increases or retention of certification to additional in-service or university course hours may have encouraged teachers to attend in-service programmes, but even so there is no guarantee that new ideas and technologies will find their way into classroom practice.

The demands upon the teacher listed earlier in this section must be addressed, if improvements in teaching and learning outcomes within the classroom or other educational settings are to be realized. In effect, enduring modification to classroom practice can only occur when the perceived needs of the teacher are satisfied and when the demands placed upon them are lifted. One could mount a convincing argument, however, that the development

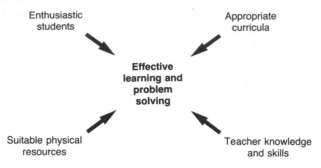

Figure 1.2 Influences on student learning outcomes

of new technologies and their marketing are increasing, rather than decreasing, the pressures on the teacher, school and the education systems. One might be forgiven for describing many of these innovations as little more than reinventions of the wheel using different coloured spokes.

It is against this background of teachers' needs that PBI was developed. Importantly, the needs of teachers have been foremost in our minds when attempting to address both theory and practical application of PBI in a way that maximizes the existing knowledge, skills and proficiencies of teachers. It is also important, however, to consider those factors which influence students' learning and problem-solving (see Figure 1.2).

FOUR IMPORTANT PROGRAMME CRITERIA

The roots of Process-Based Instruction (PBI) were established in 1980. At that time, there was a decline in teachers' confidence in the wide variety of innovative teaching and testing resources, such as the Frostig-Horne Program in Visual Perception, the Illinois Test of Psycholinguistic Abilities (ITPA), SRA kits, and behavioural (or data-based) approaches to classroom teaching. Enthusiasm was growing for those approaches that emphasized the importance of teaching children how to think. Researchers were writing about concepts such as memory strategies, metacognition and executive processes and, like many of our colleagues around the world, we also were involved in research that was concerned with how students learn and how teachers teach.

Over several years, however, it became clear that many of the methods being advocated by researchers to improve or change classroom teaching methods were ineffective, if not altogether inappropriate. Many of these approaches were often more relevant to work undertaken in the controlled climate of the psychological laboratory than to the dynamic environment of the classroom. Notwithstanding this, there were many excellent ideas and procedures that had been developed through laboratory research that were directly relevant to classroom teaching practice.

We became keenly aware that teachers were, understandably, wary of innovation for the sake of change alone, and that any new approach must take into account the way in which classrooms operate *and* be based firmly on instructional theory and application. Because of this thinking, we prescribed four criteria which PBI must satisfy. It must:

- operate in classrooms;
- operate within the regular programme of the classroom;
- focus on student involvement; and
- enable teachers and students to apply a set of principles and procedures across a wide range of learning situations.

Criterion One: Operation in classrooms, not laboratories

The first essential feature of any teaching and learning programme must be its direct application to regular classrooms. As mentioned above, much of the early research on the teaching of thinking skills was undertaken in laboratories or in similar controlled learning environments. Typically, researchers withdrew students from their classrooms on a one-to-one or small group basis, to work on a newly developed package or programme. The 'teacher' in these situations commonly used novel (often content-free) materials that were developed for the research project. The classroom teachers were infrequently involved. More likely, teachers were actively discouraged from participating in the exercise on the assumption that they would inadvertently – or deliberately – confound the study by using the new methods or materials with students who were not part of the experiment.

While many of these studies provided valuable insights about how children learn or process information in novel situations, the extent to which these skills would generalize to regular or special classroom curriculum activities was questionable. The two environments, laboratory and classroom, bear little relationship to each other. Researchers recognized the differences many years ago (see, for example, Pressley, Levin, and Bryant, 1983) but many have persisted in their exploration of micro-learning events in carefully controlled settings.

It is our belief that many of the results of laboratory-based research on instructional practice (when most factors are under the explicit control of the researcher) are not readily transferable to learning in the regular classroom (where events and interactions constantly change). We hasten to add that this does not negate the findings of empirical research. Investigators must describe the important principles of learning and problem solving, but it is essential to ensure that research results eventually translate into methods which can be applied independently of environmental factors. If all classrooms operated like laboratories, there would be numerous and obvious applications of laboratory research and we would have a few concerns – but they don't.

Criterion Two: Operation within the regular programme of the classroom

Classroom teachers, world-wide, are beset by many competing demands. There is a constant stream of:

- new curriculum documents which require introduction;
- individual education plans to be prepared and enacted in some education systems;
- new policies to be understood and implemented; and
- interruptions to teaching time during the course of the school day.

The introduction of a new teaching and learning method must not add to the existing demands of accountability and system-based teaching initiatives, such as new curricula or implementation strategies.

Some programmes designed to remediate poor student performance or to enhance students' thinking skills require teachers to add yet another component to their programme (one that may, by design, be unrelated to the curriculum). The demands of other programmes may require teachers to use specific instructional strategies that relate only to a small number of curriculum tasks or exercises. For example, teachers may present students with a strategy designed to enhance certain reading comprehension skills at the primary or secondary level, or one to assist students with a specific spelling or mathematics problem. In most cases, these specific strategies have limited application, apart from the one for which they were designed.

Programmes aimed at developing students' thinking skills must be integrated into the usual teaching practices and must transcend curriculum areas. Most importantly, they must be seen as part of the accepted teaching-learning process, integrating methods which train students to think about how they learn and problem solve using current curriculum content across subject areas. In this way, the application and generality of the methods are apparent to both teachers and students.

Criterion Three: Focus on student involvement

Researchers who have studied the time allocated to classroom instruction and to students' on- and off-task behaviours have demonstrated that there is considerable variability across groups of students (see, for example, Fields, 1991; Ysseldyke, Thurlow, Christenson, and Weiss, 1987). In some situations, children may be on-task as little as 10 to 15 per cent of the time. Our observations of children during classroom activities have confirmed that many primary school children spend a considerable amount of time off-task (watching others, talking and fiddling) irrespective of whether they have a learning problem or not. Often, the only apparent difference between children with and without a learning problem is the inability of the first group to complete the assigned task within the lesson period.

While on-task behaviour is a prerequisite for successful learning and problem-solving, classroom instruction for students rarely focuses on teaching them how to direct and monitor their school work. Some strategies, such as verbal self-instruction techniques (also called cognitive behaviour modification) involve teacher-designed and directed learning. In most situations, students make little contribution to the process, yet there is no doubt that students can design, initiate and regulate their own learning behaviour effectively. Teaching students to do this, however, requires consistent and systematic instruction. When achieved, it provides them with some degree of control over, and ownership of, the teaching–learning process. PBI leads directly to this goal.

We are not suggesting that PBI – or for that matter, any other strategy that promotes the students' involvement in learning – will lead to the elimination of all off-task behaviour. Children will still choose to be, or not to be, on-task. However, if they have a mechanism that enables them to direct their own learning behaviour, then they can determine when it is appropriate to be on- and off-task.

Criterion Four: Application of new skills within the classroom

Research concerned with the effectiveness of teaching, learning and problem-solving strategies has not provided conclusive evidence of how we can ensure that students transfer their knowledge and skills to tasks and situations removed from the training setting. Most, if not all, contemporary researchers recognize the importance of teaching generalizable skills.

The use of newly developed skills can only be achieved by making explicit the connection between the training and the task to which one wants students to generalize. In other words, we cannot assume that students are able to recognize the connections and we must show how specific skills are, or can be, made relevant to a range of activities.

In summary, our efforts to produce a programme to teach students how to become more effective learners and problem solvers were guided by these four general criteria. The programme needs to:

- operate as part of the regular classroom activities and involve the teacher directly;
- integrate instruction in how to learn and problem solve within the framework of content being presented by the teacher;
- demonstrate to students the value of their active involvement in the teaching-learning process; and
- directly address the generalization of learning and problem-solving skills and strategies so that students can clearly see the relevance of the approach.

The four criteria address some of the concerns expressed by teachers about the introduction of new or novel teaching methods. They also satisfy a number of essential features of effective instructional programmes identified by educational researchers. We now move on to outline the foundations of PBI.

WHAT PBI IS DESIGNED TO ACHIEVE

Process-Based Instruction has a developmental focus. It is designed to meet teaching objectives at two levels – what occurs in specific lessons, and what occurs across grades or developmental levels.

For a classroom teacher, PBI provides a structure into which the teaching–learning process will fit. It provides an effective strategy for guiding the learning process, irrespective of the age or ability levels of students who attend regular or mainstream classes and, in some cases, for students attending special classes.

For teachers across grades, PBI provides the backdrop for the development of students' academic and thinking skills using a consistent approach. In this sense, the backdrop is the teacher's systematic use of what we call PBI plans and the extension and refinement of the planning process as students gain knowledge, experience and skills. When students progress from grade to grade, the skills developed at one level are enhanced and extended at the next. Teachers have no need to lay the foundation of PBI at the beginning of each school year but simply continue to use methods comparable to those of other teachers.

For individual students, PBI provides a way to learn which is suited to personal learning styles, existing knowledge and skills. PBI allows students to work privately or with others, and to have control over their learning process. The teacher will still set the content, procedures and the pace of learning, but the student will have an active part to play in the process.[2]

As students progress through school, they learn planning, decision-making and problem-solving skills within the context of the curriculum. The important point is that students develop independence in making and refining plans in activities inside and outside the classroom.

THE BASES OF PBI

Up to this point, we have indicated that PBI is both a curriculum model and a teaching–learning process. The classroom practices and strategies that teachers use are the same as those already established and in common use throughout the world. We have been careful to ensure that teachers who are learning about PBI realise that they are not being asked to abandon their established, successful teaching methods. As such, PBI is compatible with existing regular classroom and special education practices and strategies.

Being sensitive to the nature of the classroom and to the process of learning is only one consideration during the formative stage of PBI. Equally important is the development of a model with a firm conceptual foundation. The theory (or perhaps more accurately, the conceptual framework) of PBI derives from the problem-solving, planning, neuropsychology and educational psychology literature. We will deal more extensively with some of the key features in Chapter 2 but it will be useful at this point to draw attention to the two key concepts with which we will be dealing, plans and planning.

Plans and planning

PBI focuses upon the teacher's use of plans to help students learn new material effectively. Teachers instruct students to use plans, to amend them to suit their needs or learning style, and to develop their own personal plans. Teachers demonstrate why planning is important in and out of the classroom and help students to become conscious of their own planning efforts. As with all PBI activities, the regular school programme and curriculum provides the instructional context.

What is a plan? In very general terms a plan is a sequence of activities or thoughts that will lead to success on a specific task. In PBI, we need to clarify what the sequence entails, and what may be meant by success. We will consider these matters in detail in Chapter 4.

What is planning? Planning is the process of developing plans for known or unknown, real or speculative tasks or problems.

Planning is a fundamental skill that every individual must develop during their lives; it has its beginning in the early school years. What the teacher may communicate about planning to a kindergarten class would be very different to the discussion that would be held with Grade 12 (sixth-form) students. Nevertheless, many classroom activities, projects and learning events can be, and often are, oriented toward planning.

This book will demonstrate ways in which plans and planning can be introduced to, and used by, students across grade and ability levels. Rather than being a static or ability-specific strategy, PBI is designed to teach students about the application of planning and problem-solving strategies – in other words, it is more than simply the use of a plan.

PBI is a way of systematically and explicitly teaching students how to learn and how to problem-solve.

THE EDUCATIONAL OBJECTIVES OF PBI

PBI has been operating in regular and special education classes for a number of years. It began as a classroom-based, teaching and learning programme, designed to raise the academic performance of teenagers who were attending special classes for students with mild intellectual disabilities.[3] At that stage, the movement toward the integration of special education students into regular (mainstream) classes had been accepted as a general principle, although the application of the principle had not been widely attempted. PBI was developed as a model that was sensitive to the importance of teaching those students how to learn, and how to learn about problem-solving. Trials took place in their special classes, providing the opportunity for the authors to refine the classroom procedures and the in-service programme for teachers. A description of this project is reported in Conway and Ashman (1992).

Within a period of 18 months following the first classroom application of PBI, acceptance of the mainstreaming philosophy in most Australian states led to the integration of students with special needs into regular programmes and to the closure of many special classes for students with mild learning problems. As a consequence of this, it became important to conceive of PBI as a regular classroom model that would accommodate students who had a wide range of abilities and skills. Only minor adjustments to the PBI procedures and of the in-service programme were required.

As a regular education programme, PBI was initially introduced into a large primary school and then into a number of other primary and secondary schools. A research project was initiated to monitor the effect of PBI on students' performances and on the impact of the procedures on the classroom environment. The benefits of using PBI in the skill areas of reading and mathematics, and on several information processing tests and level of school satisfaction were reported in Ashman and Conway (1992).

At the present time, PBI is being used in many educational settings. It has benefited from the critique of many teachers and school support staff: teachers have reported success in whole classes across all grades as well as in small group or individual programmes. Remedial, support and resource teachers have used PBI with gifted students and with those who have learning and developmental disabilities.

Because of the relatively sophisticated language and information processing demands, PBI has not been used extensively in classroom activities for students with more severe intellectual disabilities. Several teachers working with students with very low abilities, however, have used the basic concepts (i.e., plans, planning) to assist in the presentation of curriculum content and the preparation of classroom management or other programmes aimed at assisting students with their social or emotional adjustment.

Box 1.1 Some comments by teachers about Process-Based Instruction

Jill is a Grade 5 teacher in a small primary school in an outer suburb of a large city. She was introduced to Process-Based Instruction at a school staff meeting by one of the authors. At the time of this report Jill had been using PBI for about seven months.

The idea of making children more aware of how they learn seemed like a good one to me. I didn't really get a very good idea of what PBI was about or how to do it by the end of the introductory session and this was a little disappointing. Other teachers said the same thing and we all had a lot of questions but we realised that wasn't really the idea of the half-hour talk.

Our principal gave us the option of learning more about PBI and I think about eight of the 12 teachers said that they'd be interested.

The workshop was really interesting. They started by talking about some general teaching principles which were things we all know about but I'd never really put them together in the same way. It sort of gave us a framework for teaching. Then they put us to work.

At the end of the session, we were all pretty enthusiastic about trying out PBI – I actually went home and thought about how I could use plans in my lessons the next day. I can't say my first attempt was all that successful but it didn't take too long to see that I was getting through to the children better than before. What effect has PBI had? Well . . . it really *has* made a big difference to my teaching. I didn't think it was going to make that much difference, but it has. It's given me what I'd call 'a system', and I can see where I'm going from week to week. One of the good things is that how I use it is different to Clare [the other Grade 5 teacher on staff who shares the open classroom with Jill] and the others and yet we're all using the same ideas.

Darren is a secondary teacher in a very large metropolitan high school. He teaches English to children in Grades 8 through 12. Darren elected to attend a half-day workshop on PBI with 14 others and at this point had been using PBI for about six months.

To tell you the truth, I thought it was a waste of time. It just seemed impractical in the high school. Like I said, with all the content we have to get through in a lesson, it just seemed that there wasn't any time to do something like PBI. After the session, there were only a couple of us who were willing to give it a trial. I don't think we were very receptive.

Pat [a PBI trainer] talked with a few of us a couple of days after the session and we agreed to give it a go – to find ways of using PBI in our classes. I talked through what I was doing in a few lessons and we worked out how to start. I was still pretty hesitant about what the point was.

Anyhow, I gave it a go. I wasn't too sure about what I was doing, but Pat and I talked through the lesson and how I could get the kids more involved. It actually went pretty well – a lot easier than I thought.

I think the biggest problem in the high school is getting over the hurdle that because we have a lot of pressure on us to get through the syllabus, we don't have any time left to think about how the kids are learning. In the early days, I still wasn't all that sure of what I was trying to achieve, but it didn't take me too long to see that the lower kids in the class were picking up the ideas a lot faster.

Do you know one of the funny things? It sort of struck me one day when I was planning a class that I was doing things a lot differently, I mean *teaching*, to how I did it before.

WHAT TEACHERS HAVE SAID ABOUT PBI

As part of our monitoring activities associated with the use of PBI, we have collected anecdotal information from teachers and students. On the whole, teachers' responses have been very favourable. The comments in Box 1.1 are characteristic of many provided by classroom teachers.

USING PBI WITH YOUR STUDENTS

PBI is not a magic wand or silver bullet solution to all the learning problems teachers may confront in their classrooms. The PBI model will *assist* teachers to make subtle changes to their classroom practices and teaching strategies. Major, dramatic (or traumatic) changes are not characteristic of PBI classrooms. The effects that PBI have on students' performance will depend upon the way in which it is introduced to, and maintained in, the classroom. Systematic induction and consistent use will act as a catalyst for change in teaching and learning patterns.

Teachers who have used PBI over a number of years represent a diverse group of educators. The group includes teachers who are relatively new and those who have many years experience in the classroom. Some have been judged by their colleagues as highly effective in the classroom; others have expressed a self-perception of having difficulty in the teaching profession. Some have embraced PBI fully and have worked diligently to introduce and assimilate the model into their classroom as effectively as possible, while others have stated that they have used some of the ideas but have not worked seriously at full integration.

Some of the PBI teachers use traditional, didactic teaching methods in classes in which the students sit in rows, while others use discovery as their primary teaching strategy. Some have learning centres spread about the classroom, while others have special or personal study programmes for students to complete within a prescribed time. Several teachers describe themselves as behaviourists while others have adopted many of the new cognitive education methods such as reciprocal teaching, peer tutoring or strategy training.

In effect, PBI is able to encompass the breadth of teaching philosophies and strategies. Its introduction into the classroom, as for any other initiative, simply depends upon learning and practising the procedures.

In this book, we have presented the material in a way that will enable the reader to develop the knowledge and skills in a systematic way. We urge you to work through examples where they appear and to take the time to complete the brief exercises suggested. Following this process and using the materials in the Appendix will assist you to learn about PBI in the most expedient way.

WHY PROCESS-BASED *INSTRUCTION*?

Curriculum theorists have asked why we chose the word *instruction*, when our approach clearly advocates the principles of communication, collaboration and negotiation, and of ongoing review and evaluation. Our decision to use this term was taken after reviewing numerous potential titles and being unable to devise a short label for the programme that could succinctly communicate our philosophy.

Process-Based Instruction *does* imply a systematic process of providing educational experiences in which students learn. For some this may imply imparting knowledge – paying little attention to the reciprocal relationship between teacher and learner. For others it implies structuring learning experiences in which students play a large role in instructing themselves and others. PBI, as a broad teaching–learning framework, is applicable across these interpretations.

SUMMARY

PBI is a dynamic teaching–learning process that provides an instruction framework for teachers and a learning framework for students. It can be integrated into classroom practice as it is compatible with most, if not all, teaching strategies used in primary and secondary schools. PBI is not an experiment. It is a realistic teaching approach that is used by hundreds of teachers in a number of countries in special or regular classrooms and in small group or one-to-one teaching situations.

Chapter 2

Classroom dynamics

What is known about classrooms and other learning settings that will help promote effective teaching and learning?

Curriculum researchers operating within the psychological, sociological, philosophical and general education domains have focused attention on many variables that directly or indirectly affect academic achievement. In brief, psychologists have concentrated primarily upon learner characteristics and on the difficulties that some students experience in acquiring knowledge; sociologists have addressed the nature of the environment and the interpersonal dynamics which operate during learning; philosophers have concerned themselves with the issue of what information should be transmitted and who should possess it; and those interested in curriculum development and theory have formulated models which portray the relationships between learning processes, teaching methods and curriculum content.

In this chapter various factors – and the interactions between them – that contribute to successful learning and problem-solving outcomes will be considered, as these form the foundation of PBI. They include:

- the skills and abilities which the student possesses that facilitate or limit learning;
- the factors that relate to the content or the syllabus;
- those factors that occur as a function of the nature of the learning or problem-solving setting; and
- the skills and abilities of the teacher that help facilitate or limit students' learning and problem-solving success.

All classrooms share one thing in common – they support a highly complex set of interpersonal interactions. Some writers have emphasized the importance of human relationships and the socialization process that occurs within the classroom (Turnure, 1986). Others have been more inclusive, adding the interactions between teaching styles and methods, learner variables, and the nature of the situation in which learning takes place (Marsh, Price, and Smith, 1983; Tharp and Gallimore, 1988). Regardless of how we conceive of the events that occur in the classroom, it is especially important that teachers are aware of the *range* of factors and how they influence learning and problem-solving.

In this chapter, we outline four groups of factors that interact to affect successful, and unsuccessful, learning outcomes. These include those components which relate to learner competencies and skills, to the content being taught, the physical setting in which learning occurs and, finally, those which relate to the instructor.

LEARNER FACTORS

The first set of factors to consider are those related to the student who is the primary target of PBI. While there are numerous ways in which these factors can be described, we favour a simple division into three general components: knowledge, motivation and organization, which are graphically shown by the Venn diagram in Figure 2.1. We will deal with each of these divisions below.

Figure 2.1 Three factor groups associated with learning and problem-solving performance

Knowledge

Knowledge refers to:

- pieces (or units) of information – such as the distance between Paris and Beijing, the number of storeys in the Empire State Building in New York, or the current exchange rate of the Deutschemark in Singapore dollars;
- information processing strategies and their use – how to remember a telephone number for later use, how to keep ourselves on task when we get tired; and
- plans which have been developed for specific or general activities – how

to get to work during a transport strike, how to shop for groceries in the shortest time.

Our knowledge base, therefore, is a complex storehouse of information containing much of what we have learned from the time we were born (see Box 2.1).

Box 2.1 What do we know about Christmas?

The notion of Christmas will allow us to focus on the complexity of our knowledge base. We have a great storehouse of information associated with the concept. Perhaps the most basic information is that Christmas Day is the 25th of December. This is a unit of information, but it also provokes many other ideas which are stored in our memories. We can easily recall the Christian belief that Christ was born in a small town called Bethlehem, and that this town is about 15 kilometres south of Jerusalem. If you have visited the Holy Land, you may also know another way to spell the name of the town – Bayt Lahm. Each of these ideas, in turn, will stimulate many other recollections, not only those that are linked to pieces of information. Christmas, for example, also arouses attitudes (which are themselves a form of information), plans and strategies such as:

- our disposition toward holidays;
- religious precepts associated with the celebration of the birth of Christ;
- which people are expected to visit us during the Christmas period;
- when to buy the best quality food and delicacies;
- how much to spend on those who gave us presents last year; and
- many other details concerning events and experiences related to vacation times.

Every concept known to us will have a framework or network of knowledge associated with it. These are called schema.

A person's performance on any task or problem is related to the information known about it. This information can be located in three domains – what we must know before we can attempt the task (i.e., prerequisites); what information has been provided to help us perform that task; and what techniques may be known to help collect information which is not immediately available. Regardless of whether we are trying to learn the spelling of the word 'catch' or attempting to find the correct bus to take us from Rome to Florence, we need knowledge which is drawn from these same information domains.

Motivation

Motivation refers to the learner's desire to become involved, and to maintain that involvement, in learning and problem-solving activities. It relates to the learner's arousal (the state of readiness to receive and process information) and to the relevance or importance of the task to the individual. Motivation energizes and directs behaviour (Ferguson, 1976) and, hence, it is influenced by past experiences.

Success and failure both affect the way in which students approach learning activities (see e.g., Chapman, Silva, and Williams, 1984; Fennema and Myer, 1989). If children have a history of attainment with school-related tasks, then there is a greater likelihood that they will be industrious than if the majority of their experiences have been of failure.

There are a number of psychological concepts which help us to understand the causes of high and low motivation. One of these is our view of the reasons for success or failure (in other words, to what we attribute our success or failure). For example, students might attribute success on an exam to good luck, an easy test, or to the hard work they have done to learn the information on which the assessment was based. Other students who have been unsuccessful might think that they were just unlucky, or that the test was very difficult, or that they did not study sufficiently for it. Attributions provide a justification for performance and are part of the belief system we have about our learning and problem solving behaviour.

Another aspect of our belief system is the self-perception of control (or lack of control) we have over our lives. Students who believe they are in control of their environment, and who are intrinsically motivated to achieve mastery or success are generally those students who are most successful. In psychology, the term 'locus of control' is used to indicate that the person is driven by internal or external forces (i.e., internal locus of control or external locus of control).

Yet another factor influencing success in school is the emotional response that a child may have to the school experience. Children's views of the need for an education and the support offered by the school, home and community will in turn affect the effort and the outcomes of learning and problem-solving. Some subject areas engender uniformly unfavourable attitudes (e.g., mathematics and statistics) and, hence, are typically perceived as hard. A negative disposition toward a teacher (e.g., when there is a personality clash between student and teacher) may also reduce a student's enthusiasm for lessons and adversely affect their outcome. Conversely, a student may work diligently, having experienced considerable success in one or a number of subject areas, or may even choose a particular career path because of their admiration for a teacher who has inspired them.

As PBI involves students actively in the learning process, one direct outcome is a change in students' motivation toward academic activities and school. Of special concern is the change in students' perceptions of their contribution to the learning process and of their success.

Organization

The organization component allows us to adapt to new and novel learning and problem-solving activities. Adaptation is a sophisticated endeavour which draws on the planning and decision-making skills that are developed over the course of our lives. Think for a moment about how you would go about setting up and running a small, neighbourhood convenience store. What would you have to consider to achieve this goal? You would most certainly have to bring into play all your knowledge about small business operations – where to set up the business, how much capital you would need, how many people to employ, from whom you would purchase the stock, what percentage mark-up is needed to sustain the business, how many hours per week you would need to be open. These and many other important considerations would involve making decisions, setting priorities, determining appropriate methods for solving the problems which are encountered, and establishing and monitoring a set of performance indicators (e.g., profit and loss).

All of the activities noted in the paragraph immediately above involve making, enacting, and modifying plans to achieve a goal. We engage our organizational skills every day in many routine and mundane ways, not just when we are confronted with a novel task. For example, we adapt our behaviour to cope with long queues at supermarket check-outs. Our experience might suggest that we need to shop at less popular times; we might enlist the help of our spouse or a friend to speed the shopping process; or decide that the tedium of the check-out can be minimized by reading the latest magazine or TV guide. Knowing how we cope with the many situations we face is also part of the organization process.

The learning factor interactions

The Venn diagram in Figure 2.1 implies an interaction between the three components – knowledge, motivation, and organization. Without an appropriate knowledge base, sufficient motivation or the ability to organize and integrate information, our ability to perform a task successfully will be limited. In some situations, it is hard to compensate for a deficit in one area or another. For instance, poor general knowledge will usually act against a player in the game Trivial Pursuit. While the person may have high motivation or organizational competence, it is unlikely that this will help compensate for a poor knowledge of trivia. For those who do not like parlour games, a lack of application, enthusiasm, and competitive spirit can exacerbate the situation. Having little understanding of the importance of the tactic of buying property earlier in a game of Monopoly can leave a player seriously unprepared for the later stages of play.

While these are fairly simple examples, the same conditions apply in the

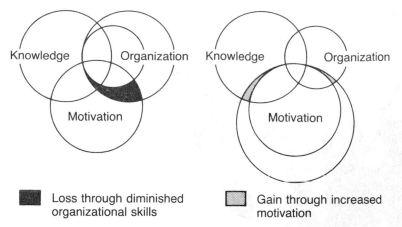

Loss through diminished organizational skills

Gain through increased motivation

Figure 2.2 The effect of changes in competencies associated with learning and problem-solving performance

classroom. Each of the cognitive domains (knowledge, motivation, organization) has been shown to have an important impact on students' learning and problem-solving. Having advanced competencies and/or positive dispositions can aid performance. If we extend the schematic view of interactions between the three domains shown in Figure 2.1, we can represent a situation of compensation, in which a strength in one area may offset a limitation in another.

The shaded area in the left diagram in Figure 2.2 shows lost potential due to reduced organizational skills, in contrast to the balanced interactions shown in Figure 2.1. It is difficult to know what this loss might mean in practical terms, as the realistic interaction of one component with another cannot be depicted adequately using a Venn diagram. The implication, however, is straightforward: one's potential to deal with the learning task or problem will be reduced. Again, in our idealized diagram, an increase in motivation – as in the diagram on the right – might compensate for some of the losses. The gains due to improvements in one area, however, may not redress the losses due to a deficit in another.

The PBI approach emphasizes the interdependence of components and the influence of these interactions on learning and problem-solving performance. The challenge for teachers is the identification of the individual student's strengths and weaknesses, and the cultivation of classroom practices that can assist all students.

CONTENT FACTORS

The second area of concern relates to the information which is being presented by the teacher. Curriculum theorists refer to the syllabus – here we prefer the term curriculum content. In addition to the knowledge that students must learn, we include the sequence in which the skill-related material is presented and the use and adaptation of materials and equipment for children who have diverse educational needs.[1] The sequencing of instruction, in particular, has been a major focus of educational research for several decades. Analysis of the development of reading, mathematics and language skills and the establishment of a hierarchy of skills within a curriculum area (called the task analysis) remains as one of the positive contributions of curriculum research undertaken during the 1960s and 1970s.

Despite the importance of task analysis, an over-reliance on packaged programs and rigid sequencing of skills has the effect of constraining the initiatives of both teacher and students as the learning circumstances change. Such an approach limits the opportunities for class members to explore tangential issues that may elicit important insights. In many cases, curriculum development activities have led to the rigid application of prescriptive teaching procedures and curriculum documents which have made teaching functionally and developmentally irrelevant.

One consistent problem that teachers confront is the mismatch between learner and content factors. It becomes especially important for the progress, or lack of it, of students with a learning difficulty. More often than not, teachers continue to progress through the syllabus without being aware that their teaching efforts are falling on deaf ears (see Box 2.2). An awareness of the way in which students deal, or are unable to deal, with an academic task will help teachers to find ways of facilitating the learning and problem-solving process.

Box 2.2 A mismatch of learner and content factors

A number of years ago, one of us was visiting a school with a support (or remedial) teacher to assist a number of teachers who had recently attended an in-service course on the use of Process-Based Instruction. One of the teachers was having difficulty with a Grade 6 boy who did not seem to be progressing in mathematics. The teacher reported: 'Scott simply can't do any of his work in mathematics. Can you spend some time with him and see if you can find out where the problem is?' The class was working on a long-division lesson and the teacher provided the notes he had been using which outlined the solution procedure. He also showed us Scott's mathematics workbook, which was more than generously littered with 'Xs' indicating incorrect answers. Scott joined us in the staff common room with his workbook and his most recent attempt at division.

The support teacher talked about Scott's sporting successes, but quickly led on to his problem with mathematics. Scott was obviously mystified by the exercise given to him by his teacher and could not even begin to suggest how he might go about solving one of the sums on the worksheet, beside which the teacher had planted a big 'X'. To his credit, he was still willing to try.

The worksheet contained a dozen long-division algorithms intended to help the students consolidate the procedures the classroom teacher had introduced in the lesson. The support teacher began by revising the procedure using the teacher's lesson notes, but it became immediately obvious that Scott was totally confused. It took little time to ascertain that Scott did not fully understand subtraction facts, let alone division. At age 13 years, the boy had the arithmetic foundations expected of a student five years his junior. How Scott had fallen so far behind his grade level is a story in itself; how he came to progress through three or four grades without remedial assistance is yet another.

An important point to consider here is that several teachers had been insensitive, if not oblivious, to Scott's lack of mathematical comprehension. The Grade 6 teacher, being the last in a long line, also failed to recognize that he was introducing concepts and procedures to the class which, while totally appropriate for Grade 6, were far beyond Scott's knowledge base. Given the dependence of the new material upon earlier arithmetic learning, there would have been no way in which Scott could have achieved success on the division exercise. His performance, zero out of twelve sums correct, would have been an excellent indicator if Scott had ever allowed the teacher to see the 'work' he had been doing during the lesson.

This case note demonstrates the serious implications for students when there is a mismatch between the learner characteristics (in this case, the prerequisite knowledge for long division) and the content being presented by the teacher. The only solution for a situation similar to the one faced by Scott is careful remediation, *if* the need is recognized.

Regardless of the apparent seriousness of Scott's learning problem, there was a happy ending. Over the years of watching the mathematical conjuring of his teachers, he had certainly picked up some ideas though they were not structured into any usable form. Scott also was a boy with some ability. After a month of skilful, individual work using PBI strategies with Scott during seven or eight class periods, the support teacher reported that the boy was progressing quickly. He had come to understand many of the basic arithmetic operations and, while considerable consolidation was still required, he would now be well on the way to catching up with the others in the class in mathematics.

CLASSROOM SETTING FACTORS

In addition to the facilitating interactions between the learner and the curriculum content, success in the classroom is also dependent upon the environment in which learning and problem-solving occurs. Some writers have referred to classroom climate or quality of life within the classroom as governing educational outcomes. Fraser (1986) identified several classroom climate issues – the cohesiveness or friction which exists within the class group, the degree of student involvement in the learning process, teacher support, clarity of class and school rules, teacher control, and innovation.

Our perception of classroom climate is a little different from Fraser's, as we separate the elements into other groupings, removing those which relate to the physical setting from others which concern the instructor. Under the present heading, we include the use of resources and space, participation in learning and problem-solving activities, and the interactions which occur within the learning environment.

Resources and space

The allocation of time to different in-class activities must be considered carefully. Through careful preparation of teaching–learning experiences, activities and resources, and organization of classroom space, the PBI teacher can ensure that students are involved in the learning process and that time is not being wasted or used inappropriately.

What resources are available to the teacher and the students will be of importance in any learning setting. Availability means not only having the equipment, but also including its use at appropriate times. Many classrooms have books and various pieces of equipment stored away in closets, cupboards and drawers. Some teachers will report that they really don't know what they have, and in some cases are not even sure for what purpose the materials can be used. Getting these items out of the cupboards and into use, or perhaps even passed on to someone who can use them, is an important first step in streamlining resources and space.

One local teacher has a wall in her classroom which is stacked high with materials which have been collected over the years: blocks, books, puzzles, boxes of toys, pencils and art materials, rope, pillows, games – you name it, she has it; and, of course, a kitchen sink! It would be hard to forget what her treasury contains as the materials are in clear view and gathered under appropriate labels. In this classroom, never a year goes by without every piece being used at least once for some activity which is designed to help the students learn in their own, individual ways.

Of course, learning is more than simply having the materials. The adage, 'You can lead a horse to water, but you can't make it drink', applies to learning. You can set up the environment to facilitate learning, but there is no guarantee that it can or will be effective in producing academic gains. In general, classrooms are arranged by teachers to reflect the way in which they teach, rather than necessarily reflecting the learning preferences of the students. Some teachers prefer to work in a classroom in which the desks are set up in rows, much the same as they were when they were at school. Other teachers set up the desks in clusters where students work in small groups. Still others organize activity centres about the classroom so that students can work at each centre in sequence on mini-projects or exercises in pairs or individually. Others prefer to use the great outdoors as their classroom and prepare lessons or learning experiences that are centred on the students' exploration of their environment.

There are some data to show that children respond to the arrangement of the space in which they work. Students in most primary classes tend to be placed around tables in groups of four to six to work on exercises set by the teacher. In Britain, the Plowden Report of 1967 justified this seating arrangement on the basis that it would enable children to learn from each other through discussion and cooperation. Wheldall (1991b) argued that while the seating arrangements employed by teachers may have changed since the release of the Plowden Report, the work required of children remained largely individually based and talk at tables tended to be unrelated to the academic activities on which the children were supposed to be engaged.

Wheldall (1991b) reported an earlier study that he and colleagues had undertaken which examined the changes in students' productivity when seating arrangements were varied. After observing a number of classes for two weeks in which children sat around tables, the arrangement was changed into the more traditional rows, then returned to the group pattern two weeks later. Students' on-task behaviour rose around 15 per cent when they were placed in rows and fell by the same amount when they returned to sitting around tables. Some children's performance rose by over 30 per cent in the row configuration and some even complained about having to work again in groups. Wheldall emphasized that he was not advocating a back to rows position, but that teachers need to vary the classroom setting to suit the nature of the exercise. We would extend Wheldall's conclusion by suggesting that the teachers also need to vary the classroom setting to suit the preferred learning style of individual students.

Each of these alternative learning settings has advantages and disadvantages. If there is a problem, however, it will come as a result of the incompatibility of the teaching setting with the students' preferred learning style, that is, from the interaction between the learner and setting factors. Some students, for example, will work productively in small groups, others might prefer the seclusion of their desk within a row of others, while still others might find that the variation of exercises available in activity centres will sustain their interest and involvement during the school day. Students who understand that their success is dependent on their own efforts may not choose to work with other children in small groups (see Webb, 1985) while others, who are unable to concentrate or who appear hyperactive, may be the curse of peers and a teacher who has chosen activity centres as the sole learning forum.

Participation

Participation refers to students' involvement in the instructional process and to the notion within PBI of the student as an active modifier of instruction, rather than a passive recipient of it. Many students learn to accept instruction passively; they are reinforced for waiting for teacher-initiated, monitored, and reinforced learning, rather than for taking an active role in the learning process. Many teachers recognize that students who have learning problems spend a great deal of their day avoiding the tasks which the teacher has set for them. Others also acknowledge that this behaviour is not limited to children with learning problems!

Observations of children working within any classroom support the perception that much learning time is wasted in the course of a school day. Researchers who have examined time on-task have reported that some students, notably those with a learning difficulty, spend as little as eight minutes per hour on-task. Researchers at the Schonell Special Education Centre at The University of Queensland found that students with a learning difficulty who are attending regular classes spent about the same time as other students engaged in non-productive activity (Ashman, van Kraayenoord, and Elkins, 1992). The only difference between the two groups was that one group generally completed the assigned task or exercise (the regular students) while the other did not (the students with a learning difficulty).

In more intensive learning settings, one would expect to see more of the students' time on-task. This seems to be the case (Fields, 1991; Haynes and Jenkins, 1986), but there is still a substantial amount of student and teacher activity which is non-academic. Fields (1991), for example, reported a study in which observations were made of 84 reading lessons being presented by support teachers. His data showed that of an average 33-minute reading lesson, four minutes were spent by students waiting for instructions. Academic activities other than reading (e.g., writing summaries, spelling drills) accounted for nearly three minutes; management occupied just over five minutes, direct reading instruction accounted for slightly less than nine minutes and indirect reading some 12 minutes. Almost 40 per cent of the time was not devoted to reading – the academic focus of the lesson.

A number of studies have also been directed toward increasing students' participation, through the use of such teaching strategies as asking questions, peer tutoring, and offering support to peers (Ladd, 1981; Strain, Odom, and McConnell, 1984). Having students develop their own solutions to problems reduces their reliance on the suggestions or solutions of others – an important consideration for children with a mild intellectual disability (Ellis, 1986). Changing the way in which students act in class can also lead to the development of positive attitudes and feelings toward themselves and to school. These subjective aspects of emotion have a greater influence on academic achievement than is commonly accepted (Morsink, Soar, Soar, and Thomas, 1986).

Interactions

The large proportion of the time in which children are in class is spent in observing or interacting with peers, or waiting to be told what to do. As

Box 2.3 A mismatch of learner and classroom setting factors

Julie-Anne was a 12-year-old attending a regular class in a large primary school. Her parents were both professional people who not only prized academic achievement but also had high, though (they believed) realistic, expectations for the futures and careers of all of their four children. They recognized that Julie-Anne was much brighter than others of her age and they believed in public schooling as a means of providing her with a broadly based education.

The class teacher was a progressive educator. She read widely and knew of the new and contemporary trends in education. She believed that children needed to interact with their peers to gain the most out of the learning experiences which she assigned. Before introducing small-group learning procedures within her classroom, she decided to prepare a sociogram and explained to the children that she was going to make seven or eight groups in which they would work over the course of the year. She asked the students to list three people with whom they would like to work, and one with whom they would not like to work. She drew up the sociogram and formed the groups based upon her findings.

Julie-Anne was a popular girl and was a favourite choice of many of the children, even some of the boys. To the teacher, it seemed that Julie-Anne would fit into almost any group, so she devoted her energies to matching up the other children before assigning the girl to her group.

Julie-Anne was not very enthusiastic about working with other children. From experience, she knew that she didn't think like many of her peers and would have preferred to work with one boy only, Robert, whom she recognized as being more like her than others in the class. The teacher rejected this suggestion when Julie-Anne put it to her.

It was not long before Julie-Anne was unhappy with her group experiences. She was much more interested in completing her work than the other three children, and she did not initiate much contact with them. They were very diligent about including her in their discussions, most of which were unrelated to the task on which they were supposed to be working.

Over a period of some weeks, Julie-Anne became less productive and more dissatisfied with school. Eventually, her mother visited the teacher to discuss the situation, as Julie-Anne had talked about the way in which her group was operating and her changing attitude to school.

This story also had a happy ending. The teacher was very receptive to the mother's enquiries and talked at length about her philosophy of teaching. She agreed that Julie-Anne did not seem to be working well with others in the group. Eventually, she made Robert and Julie-Anne into a two-person work group, and both gained much from each other.

The point here is that some settings assist students to learn more effectively than others. Remaining flexible in the way in which resources and space are used is one way of moving toward accommodating the variations in learner characteristics which are to be found in any mainstream classroom.

with other classroom setting factors, these interactions can facilitate or restrict learning and problem-solving. Placing students in work groups is one way in which teachers try to maximize the learning opportunities in the classroom. The effectiveness of groups, however, is dependent upon the industrious nature of the children (see Box 2.3) and the extent to which competition or collaboration is encouraged in the classroom.[2] Several writers have examined the dynamics which operate within student work groups and they have found that ability and gender are two factors which affect productivity. Webb (1984, 1985), for example, found that having students of approximately the same ability level did not lead to very efficient work practices – members asked each other many questions but they tended to receive few responses. Students in mixed ability groups were more likely to respond to each other's questions, enabling the group as a whole to work toward the achievement of the academic goal.

Gender also affects the form of interactions in class groups. Where there are more males than females in a group, males tend to focus their attention on other males, ignoring their female peers. When there were more females than males, the females also give their attention to the males in the group in preference to their same-sex peers. When the gender is balanced, the interaction patterns are similarly balanced (Beatty and Troster, 1987; Lockheed, 1985).

Each of the three components described above (resources, participation, interactions) affects the character and quality of the learning environment which, in turn, has a substantial effect on children's academic performance. Perhaps more important is the often forgotten point that it is not simply the structure of the classroom, neither is it the competencies of the children, nor the way in which the academic material is presented which leads to student success in the classroom. It is the complex set of interactions between these factors which dictate the outcomes. There is, however, one further important element in this complex equation: the teacher.

INSTRUCTOR FACTORS

It goes without saying that the teacher plays a key role in children's learning. While the teacher has control over the decisions relating to the content and setting, in this section we are concerned only with the manner in which instruction is provided, how feedback is given and how personal attributes, qualities and attitudes contribute to students' education.

It would not be difficult to draw up a list of ideal teacher characteristics. This might include a caring, supportive nature, enthusiasm for the job, and respect for the rights and views of others, to name just a few. These are the building blocks of the belief-structures that teachers develop about their classroom practice. These beliefs become translated into dispositions and skills such as:

- the teacher's style (e.g., demeanour, the language the teacher uses with children, and competence in controlling the children's classroom behaviour); and

- how the teacher prefers to present work to the children (e.g., emphasizing group work, a chalk-and-talk didactic teaching approach, discovery learning methods, peer tutoring or cooperative learning systems, negotiation with children about what is to be learned and how).

Take a minute or two to think about your style and preferred instructional strategies.

Teachers' attitudes are often overlooked as important contributors to classroom dynamics. An attitude is a learned disposition to react in a predictable way to certain people, situations, objects or ideas. In some cases, teachers view their role as that of informants, with the duty of presenting information to a naïve or novice group of recipients. The notion of informant carries with it assumptions about the responsibilities of those in the teaching–learning setting.

Perhaps the most important assumption relates to the division of the responsibility for giving and receiving information. Certainly, it is the teacher who has the responsibility for presenting the information and it is the student who must learn it. When learning or comprehension does not occur, culpability is often attributed to the learner's inadequate ability or attitude. It is not uncommon to overhear staff room conversations which go something like this:

Teacher 1: 'Did you have Aaron last year?'

Teacher 2: 'Yes, he was a handful. I don't think he caught on to much of anything I said. He had a real chip on his shoulder, too – he comes from a single parent home, you know? I hear his father used to beat him quite a lot.'

Teacher 1: 'I've had a lot of trouble with him this year too. He's really well behind everyone else in the class. He won't settle down to work when he's supposed to and won't pay any attention to me when I tell him to get to work. I've sent him out of the class two or three times because he wouldn't stop arguing with me. The more it went on, the more other children were starting to act up as well. I asked Sally [the counsellor] to see him, but I don't think it had much effect. I'm pretty sure he's learning-disabled.'

Teacher 2: 'I had a talk to his mother last year about that, after I talked to Miriam – who had him the year before last. The mother wasn't much help. She thought he was bright enough because he got into lots of mischief at home. In the end, I just let him do whatever he wanted to in the class so he wouldn't disrupt everyone else. That worked pretty well.

'I had his brother a couple of years ago before you came – Robert was his name – he was exactly the same. I gave up with him too. As far as I know he never amounted to anything. Aaron's going to finish up the same way.'

The names of the children and the problems being discussed by teachers will vary, but the sentiments expressed in the interaction above will be very familiar. It is implied that the reason for Aaron's (and Robert's) classroom behaviour is poor family history, low ability, and disruptive behaviour brought on by a lack of interest in learning. Culpability is assumed to rest with the student. The teacher has tried all he or she could; nothing worked, and the best strategy is simply to ignore the problem and it may go away.

While we recognize that there are many students who test the endurance and the ingenuity of teachers beyond what could reasonably be expected, in the scenario above, the teachers appear to have abrogated their responsibility for Aaron's academic progress. If a student seems unable to learn, we must first look at what we – the instructors – are doing to support the current situation. It is certainly difficult to be critical of our own performance and behaviour, but professional growth comes more from an acceptance of our fallibility and preparedness to change, than from one of infallibility and knowledge of what is right.

It is the teacher's responsibility to ensure that all factors which contribute to students' performance and progress are explored, before looking for release from what we might call the duty of care. This means trying alternative ways of transmitting knowledge to the student, seeking ways of enhancing motivation, teaching organizational skills, and changing the learning setting so that it is more consistent with the student's preferred learning style that was discussed earlier in this chapter.

Placing the responsibility on the teacher for the learners' performance is a major obligation, one which teachers may find difficult to accept in its entirety. They might argue that the educational experience of the child may be such that it will mitigate against *any* educational intervention, regardless of the enthusiasm and skill of the teacher. We have argued elsewhere (in Ashman and Conway, 1989) that it is the teacher's duty to evaluate the way in which students learn as part of the ongoing process of instruction. They must focus attention on the way in which students deal with the curriculum, the learning setting, and with the teacher as well, especially when the learning process appears to be faltering.

Some restructuring of teaching style may be needed to ensure that the content is presented in a way which is consistent with the student's knowledge framework. In other words, the teacher must make clear to the student how the task can be undertaken so that it leads to success.

Teaching–learning process emphasizes the interdependency of those involved in the acquisition and transfer of knowledge and skills. Both teacher and learner have responsibilities for the success of the outcomes.

A change in the commonly accepted view of the term 'instruction' – that implies only the presentation of information – is needed. In its place the term, teaching–learning process is preferred.

SUMMARY

In this chapter, four groups of factors have been outlined that contribute to success or failure of learning and problem-solving in most, if not all, educational settings. We have not catalogued all aspects of each group of factors, but have highlighted several major points which define each group. Researchers have tended to concentrate their energies on the study of individual elements and the effects that these have on learners and their endeavours to understand the nature of learning and problem-solving. What occurs in education, however, is infrequently the result of one agent only – many contribute to the final outcome. It is important, therefore, for teachers to be sensitive to those factors and to seek an understanding of how they, individually and as a group, affect the learning behaviour of all children, separately and as a group. Understanding what takes place in the classroom is the first step toward changing it.

Chapter 3

Human learning and problem-solving

What is known about instructional methods and strategies that will help develop an effective teaching and learning approach?

Chapter 2 focused on several of the many factors which influence teaching effectiveness and positive learning outcomes. It did not deal with teaching practice *per se*, that is, how to present lessons or to manage students' classroom behaviour. Of course, these are essential skills which every teacher must possess. However, this book is primarily concerned with *maximizing* school-based learning and problem-solving through the application of Process-Based Instruction which is a blend of information processing theory and sound classroom practice. It is, therefore, important to overview some of the terms and concepts used by researchers, writers and educators to describe how learning and problem-solving occurs. This chapter will:

- define the concept of learning;
- introduce several ideas which help to explain how learning and problem-solving occurs;
- describe a number of instructional programmes which have used information processing as their theoretical foundation; and
- outline the major concepts used in Process-Based Instruction.

WHAT IS LEARNING?

Human learning is concerned generally with acquiring knowledge and skills. We talk about learning how to read, how to play the piano and how to drive a car. We learn about the world around us, about technology, science and society, and about prejudices, morality and values. We also learn that there are vast individual differences in the ability of people to learn and to reason.

Several decades ago psychologists realized that it is very difficult to define learning in a precise way (Hilgard and Bower, 1966). As the years have passed, the problem of clarifying the nature of learning still has not really been resolved. Our colleagues who have adopted a behavioural viewpoint describe learning as a relatively permanent process that results from practice and is reflected in changes in performance. Their explanation of how learning occurs is based upon the consequences of specific behaviours and how important these consequences are to us. Behaviourists argued that when certain environmental conditions occur, learning will take place, apparently independent of any conscious, human involvement. B.F. Skinner, the 'father of behaviourism', maintained this position up to his death.

From a different perspective, learning can be described in terms of the thought processes that occur within our brains. From this viewpoint, to the observable outcomes of learning we add the processes of learning, which involve:

- paying attention to what is to be learned;
- understanding the relationship between the information being presented and what is already known;
- understanding how learning occurs;
- controlling the rate and quality of learning; and
- being aware that learning has taken place.

This second approach to learning is very relevant to classroom practice as it takes into account the role of the person in the educational process. We usually refer to it as the cognitive or information-processing approach to learning; cognitive processing involves the intellectual activity known as cognition.

WHAT IS COGNITION?

In this book the word 'cognition' is used quite extensively in the discussion of the process of learning, so it will be worthwhile to explain what the word means. The first place we might look is in a dictionary. The *Shorter Oxford English Dictionary* defines cognition as 'the action or faculty of knowing; knowledge, consciousness . . . or the product of such an action' (p. 337). Other writers have referred to cognition as any process which allows an organism to know and be aware. It involves perceiving, reasoning, conceiving and judging (Wolman, 1973). From this more precise psychological definition, we arrive at the term 'information processing'.

Information processing is often used interchangeably with cognition. Information processing emphasizes the *way* in which humans think and learn through the acquisition, organization, storage, retrieval and evaluation of information, concepts and reasoning skills. Hence, learning involves the manipulation of information being presented to us in such a way that it is integrated into our existing knowledge base (that is, what we know already). To learn, we need to be active, constructive processors of information rather than passive receivers of knowledge. In other words, to learn the meaning of an idea or how to do something, we need to work at it.

While we cannot directly observe how information is being processed in our brains, we can gather information about what people do when they are processing information and what the outcome of this processing is. From these observations, psychology researchers have described the way in which people learn and remember by constructing models that can be tested experimentally.[1] These are based upon inferences about learning, memory and (more generally) thinking and they describe the relationships between cognitive processes or operations, effort and outcomes. Most models of cognition also take into account the learner's strategies and the manner in which memory and other thinking processes are used in learning and problem-solving.

Memory

Memory, recall and recollection are words in everyday use. Memory relates to the ability of living organisms to think about (relive) past experiences. Researchers have claimed that memory has four components

- learning – how we gain new information and skills;
- retention – how we store the new knowledge;
- recall – how we remember the knowledge when we need it; and
- recognition – how we determine which information is needed and when.

Many of the early ideas about memory were developed from studies of short- and long-term memory, in which researchers examined how long it took their subjects to learn and forget novel pieces of information. Much of the early writing seemed to describe memory as a place in the brain where information was held and, of course, sometimes lost.

Contemporary views of memory, mainly established through the study and results of electrical stimulation of the brain through an open skull, and through work with amnesics, have convinced researchers that memories are not held in any one place in the brain.[2] Rather, memory involves complex electrochemical changes in the brain creating electrical networks which reflect what we see in our mind's eye. This suggests the dynamic and strategic nature of memory and, hence, learning.

Strategies

Strategies refer to the many ways in which we take in, store and retrieve information (called 'coding', in psychology) – hence we have memory strategies, cognitive strategies, coding strategies, and information-processing strategies. These terms mean much the same. A strategy, therefore, is a way of organizing and/or integrating information – information received from our surroundings or already stored in our brain.

As we grow and interact with the world around us, we learn that there are a number of strategies which help us to process information. In some learning and problem-solving situations, one strategy may work for us better than another. Indeed, certain strategies are better suited to improving our understanding of academic tasks and skills, while others are more suited to the learning of facts or complex information. Several of the more common strategies, such as rehearsal, chunking, categorization, verbal elaboration and even note-taking, are described in Moely *et al.* (1986) and in numerous other places.

It is common to find huge individual differences in the effectiveness of specific strategies or strategy sets. In other words, some strategies work better for some people. This is particularly important to remember when dealing with students in mixed ability, regular classrooms.

Many memory strategies have very specific purposes (e.g., rehearsal) while others have more general application (e.g., behaviour monitoring) and these are often called executive strategies because they govern the operation of groups of strategies or sequences of behaviour or cognition.

Executive strategies

Most models of cognition include a component that is called the 'executive'. This is a hypothetical controlling agent or process that can intellectually assess the activities occurring within the brain. In other words, the executive allows us to obtain an overview of our thought processes (see Figure 3.1). It has several functions:

- predicting limitations in information-processing capacity;
- maintaining an awareness of the self-instruction activities and their value;
- maintaining awareness of both problems being faced and strategies being applied; and
- monitoring of problem-solving operations.

In brief, the executive acts to control our information-processing activities (Brown, *et al.*, 1983). Self-checking and keeping-place are two executive processes which are used quite often. For example, as we were preparing this manuscript, we were continually monitoring the inclusion of unusual terms to ensure that they had been defined.

One important executive strategy involves our knowledge of how we think and learn. The term 'metacognition' was introduced in the 1970s to describe the awareness of cognition (that is, a person's understanding of the information-processing involved in complex tasks). Over the years, it has taken on a broader meaning than when first defined in the mid-1960s. These days, metacognition also includes competence in planning, monitoring, self-questioning and self-directing activities. Terms commonly associated with metacognition in teaching practice include 'planning to make a plan', 'stop-check' and 'knowing when, where, and how to remember'. Hence, metacognition relates to all stages of problem-solving and academic endeavours, such as:

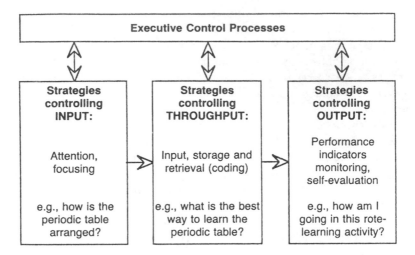

Figure 3.1 A diagrammatic representation of the relationship between executive control processes and information-processing activities using a task involving the learning of the periodic table of elements in chemistry

- recognizing the need for a strategy;
- evaluating the task requirements;
- searching for the availability of an appropriate strategy within the person's repertoire of strategies;
- executing the strategy; and
- monitoring the effectiveness of the strategy (Campione and Brown, 1978).

Many of the early studies which dealt with executive processes were based upon the presumed need to make information-processing more efficient through memory control processes called 'metamemory'. Studies by Brown and her colleagues in the late 1970s were the first attempts at metamemory training with students with mild intellectual disabilities (Brown and Barclay, 1976). A major feature of these interventions was the emphasis on teaching children how to develop and use general skills such as checking and self-monitoring. Many of the training programmes used novel, laboratory tasks rather than real-life activities and the results of the studies demonstrated obvious age-related differences. Not surprisingly, older children were more competent in using general strategies in their problem-solving activities than their younger peers.

The early studies of metacognition are of historical importance because they guided researchers to reconsider the complexity of human thought. Many reports, however, disclosed that students were unable to transfer the use of strategies from the task on which they were trained to similar tasks which required the use of the same skills. While investigators emphasized the need for student involvement in learning, children did not seem to recognize the importance of using specific strategies for specific tasks or the value of a certain strategy to a cluster of tasks (Brown and Palincsar, 1982). Notwithstanding the generally disappointing results, many researchers were confident that strategy and metastrategy training held the key to improving learning and problem-solving behaviour. This led to a re-evaluation of teaching methods and materials and a perceived need to link strategy and metastrategy use to specific teaching activities and curriculum tasks.

In the next section a number of instructional programmes are outlined which have incorporated cognitive concepts and principles. When reading through this section, you will note that researchers have given little attention to factors which may contribute to successful learning outcomes other than those in the cognitive domain.[3] At least some of them have ignored the interaction of factors that were considered in Chapter 2 and which are fundamental to PBI (the learner, the content, the context in which learning occurs, and the teacher).

THE ROLE OF COGNITIVE RESEARCH IN EDUCATION

In the 1960s and 1970s, many teaching and learning approaches were developed which had information-processing as their foundations. Early studies of information-processing capabilities were mainly concerned with teaching children how to use specific strategies or metastrategies, and typically involved withdrawing students from their regular classes for training. Changes in students' performances on a select group of tests often demonstrated what researchers called success; in other words, children demonstrated an ability to use strategies for a particular purpose, although few gains were ever reported on academic skills and most gains were of short duration. Teachers often expressed some frustration that very few, if any, of these changes were noticed in the children's classroom behaviour subsequent to the cognitive intervention. Occasionally researchers stated explicitly that they were not seeking gains in academic performance, only in students' thinking ability. The lack of practical application was a major stumbling block to any widespread adaptation of new procedures for inclusion in regular teaching practice.

In their defence, many researchers at that time were not concerned with the *application* of cognitive strategies to academic skills, such as reading and arithmetic, but in the nature of the learning and problem-solving processes. In other words, researchers were trying to understand how learning and problem-solving occurred and in confirming and refuting their beliefs by experimentation. When researchers' attention was on changing school-related performance, their focus was often on the correction of deficits being experienced by students with a learning difficulty or an intellectual disability. In general, success was even more limited in these studies.

By the late 1970s a number of cognitive remedial teaching models had been developed. Some were adaptations of behavioural approaches, while others derived from the strategy and metastrategy training paradigms. Two categories of cognitive education approaches can be identified – cognitive behavioural approaches, and those that emphasize strategy and/or metacognitive training. Not surprisingly, advocates were often very optimistic about the benefits which would accrue to students if teachers adopted one approach or another.

Cognitive behavioural approaches

From the late 1940s to the mid-1970s, behaviourism played a major role in the advancement of psychological and educational practices. The primary focus was on students' behaviour and the belief that the teacher's role was to organize the environment to evoke a specific response. Behavioural methods and behaviour management procedures were considered to be an integral part of classroom practice, although the perception of behaviourism as a controlling method, driven by data collection and the manipulation of children's learning, led to the decline of pure behaviourism by the late 1970s. In its place, behavioural approaches were developed which included the belief that both cognition and physiology played interactive roles in cause and effect. The introduction of cognition to a behavioural model assisted in the explanation of behaviour when observable responses were not obvious. For example, beliefs and expectations can influence what we notice around us as a result of our awareness or conscious thought. In a similar way, external events may have a direct influence on our behaviour and physiology. A poor diet, for instance, may be the direct cause of irritability associated with hypoglycemia.

From these beliefs came the cognitive behavioural approaches to instruction. Whereas behavioural interventions focused on the condition of learning and content, cognitive approaches dealt with the internal processing strategies available to the learner. See Box 3.1 for a brief overview of one cognitive behavioural approach.

Approaches that emphasize strategy training

With the expansion of the strategy training literature, came the development of intervention programmes based specifically on the training of information-processing strategies and metastrategies (e.g., metacognition). These were aimed at different target groups. Some have been used predominantly with students with learning problems, while others have application in regular classrooms. All focus on teaching students to use strategies which can be applied to a number of areas including academic, social, and general thinking, but all place their primary emphasis on promoting strategy use and generalization rather than on developing special academic skills such as reading or mathematics. (A brief overview of one programme is given in Box 3.2.[4])

Box 3.1 Cognitive behavioural instruction through verbal self-instruction training

Cognitive behavioural instruction seeks to modify behaviour by changing the person's thought patterns about how knowledge is acquired and used (Shuell, 1986). It is based upon an acceptance that both environmental and personal factors are important to the process of learning. Unlike the earlier 'pure' behaviourists, advocates of cognitive behavioural instruction emphasize the learner's responsibility for learning rather than simply the efforts of an outside trainer in moving them from dependence to independence in learning. The mental activities of self-monitoring, self-checking and self-evaluation are the strategies most commonly applied (i.e., self-instruction techniques).

The earliest cognitive behavioural studies were attributed to Meichenbaum and his colleagues (Meichenbaum and Goodman, 1971; Meichenbaum and Asarnow, 1978). Their verbal self-instruction approach was based on the proposition that a teacher can guide students through a series of self-instruction steps to help them learn and problem-solve. For example, a student may learn to verbalize the process involved in spelling a new word as: 'First, I will look at the word. Then I will try to break it into smaller parts . . .', and so on. Through systematic training, self-instructions become internalized by the student as part of a repertoire of learning strategies. Concurrently, the teacher's role becomes less directive and more supportive. Cognitive behavioural training typically follows a five-step sequence:

1 Cognitive modelling – the instructor models the self-instructions;
2 Overt external guidance – students perform the task while the teacher provides the instructions;
3 Overt self-guidance – students perform the task while instructing themselves aloud;
4 Faded overt guidance – students whisper the instructions while completing the task;
5 Covert self-instruction – students perform the task while using internal (private) language.

The training sequence is distinctly behavioural. The strategy training aspect allows the student to learn an appropriate strategy to deal with specific problems. In more recent developments of the verbal self-instruction approach, educators have placed greater emphasis on the generation of strategies by the student rather than by the teacher.

Box 3.2 Strategies Program for Effective Learning/Thinking (SPELT): an outline

SPELT was described first in Peat *et al.* (1989) and is generally characteristic of many cognitive education approaches which are intended for use at the whole-classroom level. It is a 'modification of the work of Deschler [sic]/ Schumaker and their associates . . . [which has been] adapted to suit the instructional environment and needs of youngsters in the regular classroom as compared to its original application with learning disabled adolescent population' (p. 103).

SPELT has three phases: Phase 1 involves the direct teaching of programme-recommended, teacher-identified, or teacher-generated strategies. These alert students to the existence of cognitive strategies and demonstrate that the efficient, goal-oriented use of strategies will improve the acquisition, retrieval, application and appreciation of those strategies. The key feature of the phase is metacognitive empowerment which is derived from students' recognition of performance outcome under conditions of strategy-use and strategy non-use (Marfo and Mulcahy, 1991).

Phase 2 focuses on the maintenance and generalization of strategies learned during Phase 1. The teacher systematically introduces the strategies taught in one subject area to other subjects, settings and situations. The authors claim that the process of adapting strategies to other applications will facilitate students' modification or extension of the initial strategies taught during the first phase.

In Phase 3, students will have acquired a large repertoire of strategies which have been effective in various tasks, and the classroom dialogue is directed toward the generalization of class-developed strategies and the further refinement of strategy applications. This is said to allow students to operate with little teacher involvement.

SPELT is introduced and maintained through an emphasis on learning specific strategies for specific activities and skill areas. Peat *et al.* document 44 strategies as a summary list of those used in the programme. These include:

- a concentration strategy for self-monitoring of inattentive behaviour;
- Flow-charting as an organizational/planning device for breaking a process into steps;
- the ODD strategy, which is a device to make children aware of their degree of emotional discomfort using a drawing of a thermometer scaled 0–100;
- the SQ3R textbook chapter strategy, which is a study strategy helpful for comprehending large volumes of material; and
- PMI, which is a strategy used to explore an issue by listing all the positive, negative and interesting points.

SPELT emphasizes the use of teacher-selected, teacher-directed strategies. As in Deshler's SIA, there appears to be little instructional flexibility in the first phase of SPELT for student-oriented learning and problem-solving and little consideration given to individual differences in student learning and problem-solving. Nevertheless, the authors state that the programme focuses on general strategies as well as social, mathematics, reading and knowledge-acquisition, memory, study skills and time-management, mood-setting and metacognitive strategies.

Peat *et al.* provide many links in their rationale to other strategy-training research and the inclusion of specific strategies within the programme. The approach, however, seems to ignore the considerable body of literature which refers to the ill-advised practice of imposing learning strategies on students without considering their specific needs and preferred learning styles.

Other cognitive education programmes have been developed for specific academic skills. Reading, spelling and mathematics are the three areas that have come under closest scrutiny. Two well-known approaches to reading are worthy of comment here.

Informed Strategies for Learning[5] was designed to help classroom teachers increase their pupils' awareness of:

- which strategies are effective for reading;
- how the strategies work; and
- when and why the strategies help in reading.

The programme concentrates on skimming, inferring and summarizing strategies and consists of 20 instructional modules of three lessons each. The first lesson in each module describes and demonstrates the strategy, the second focuses upon the students' involvement and responsibility for being an active learner, and the third is a bridging lesson in which the strategies are used in a reading activity outside the classroom (such as the library or reading for recreation). A limitation of this approach is its application to a single curriculum area only.

Reciprocal teaching is a well-publicized metacognitive strategy which targets summarizing, questioning, predicting, and clarifying strategies to improve children's reading comprehension. It has components which are common to many existing methods and procedures which have been designed to teach cognitive skills. A primary focus is the provision of opportunities for students to practise the use of specific strategies, and to monitor and evaluate their effectiveness.[6]

Many of the reading comprehension strategy training programmes have two main conceptual bases in common: scaffolding and self-questioning. Scaffolding refers to the provision of a temporary, adjustable support provided by the teacher to assist students to develop and extend their skills in the early phases of instruction. The procedure involves a learning game in which children take turns in leading a dialogue about the material presented in a reading text. The teacher guides the students in how to prompt for information, how to summarize and modify the activity to help recall. In the process, the teacher provides both instruction and support for children during the learning of the strategies, and progressively withdraws that support as they become more competent in summarizing, questioning, predicting and clarifying the material which has been read. As questioning and other learning skills develop and begin to facilitate learning, the scaffold (teacher support) is gradually removed. This withdrawal of direction enables the transfer of responsibility for the instructional input from the teacher to the students (Rogoff and Gardner, 1984).

As is the case for many other programs, the academically-oriented cognitive instruction schemes have been enthusiastically promoted and studied. Advocates have claimed that as students develop their information-processing skills, they become more active learners and collaborators and show distinct improvements in academic or other intellectual pursuits.

HAVE COGNITIVE EDUCATION PROGRAMMES WORKED?

Throughout the world there may be hundreds of classroom-based, cognitive education programmes in operation, based upon cognitive behavioural methods, strategy training, or metastrategy training principles. The approaches to which we have referred above are only some of the more prominent programmes which have been reported in the educational and psychological literature, and the answer to the question 'Do cognitive education programmes work?', at least for these, is a reserved 'Yes'.

There seems little doubt that the content-oriented or skill-based programmes are successful. For example, there are many reports in the literature attesting to the success of Reciprocal Teaching, although there are few that reveal incontestable, positive outcomes of the more comprehensive programmes such as SPELT. Perhaps the most positive statement that could be made about many of the more popular programmes is that they may assist some, if not all, students to develop their information processing, learning and problem-solving skills. They may also assist some teachers, though obviously not all, to become more effective or efficient in the classroom.

If cognitive education programmes have worked, why?

In answering this question, it might be useful to look briefly at some similarities in, and differences between the approaches described above. Some of the similarities include:

- an emphasis on the need for students to be actively involved in the learning and problem-solving process;
- a focus on teaching students how to use a range of strategies;
- the inclusion of phases in which students must apply their newly acquired skills;
- the promotion of the transfer of responsibility for learning and problem-solving from the teacher to the student;
- the prescriptive nature of the programs, specifying which strategies the students must learn in order to deal with the problem or the learning event at hand; and
- the requirement for the teacher to be responsible for deciding what strategy or strategies apply to the task, and determining at what rate learning occurs.

While the points made immediately above show that there are a number of similarities, the various approaches are also different in a number of ways:

- Some, like reciprocal teaching, are conceptually fairly simple and easily incorporated by a teacher into the normal classroom programme at the primary and secondary levels. Others require an additional component to the regular school programme for training in the use of information-processing strategies.
- Some, like verbal self-instruction, require little training once the basic concept has been learned by the teacher, while for others, extensive

(and expensive) in-servicing is required before teachers are considered sufficiently skilled to use the programme appropriately.

- Some have a provision for student input into the decision-making process, while others effectively reduce the opportunities for students to apply their individual learning style or preference to the task.
- Some, like Informed Strategies for Learning, are based upon a published programme, while others (e.g., SPELT) depend upon the skill of the teacher to introduce a strategy when it is considered appropriate.

Commitment to a belief in the efficacy of a programme is a powerful agent of change. If a teacher is enthusiastic about a particular method, possesses the relevant teaching skills, and has a clear view of the processes involved and of programme goals, it is likely that students will derive some benefits from it. It may be hard to judge whether the perceived (or observed) student gains are directly attributable to the programme or simply to an increase in teacher and student motivation: a by-product of teacher enthusiasm and diligent instruction.

Having said this, there are a number of reasons why cognitive education programmes would be effective. Perhaps the most important reason is the attention that is given to students' involvement in classroom teaching and learning activities and processes. This feature, common to most programmes, is based upon the belief that students need to be actively involved if they are to understand what is to be done and why, and for them to gain experience with the concepts and processes being taught.

A second reason for the apparent success of cognitive education programmes is their application of processes which underlie learning. All programmes address strategic and metastrategic skills, affective aspects of learning – such as motivation – and the majority of them also focus on discrete academic and non-academic skills which have clearly defined steps. Most also emphasize the importance of the teacher's involvement as a mediator of student learning, either through one-to-one interactions with students or at the level of the whole class. In some cases an attempt has been made to bridge the gap between regular and special education by providing applications which are appropriate for students with diverse skills and abilities, notably through the use of scaffolding techniques.

Some matters that have remained unresolved

Most, if not all, of the well-known programmes have their detractors. For the most part, critics of cognitive education approaches have not challenged the conceptual bases but have argued that there has been little conclusive evidence to show that they work. Others have suggested that inconsistencies in application make convincing evidence difficult to gather (see Wong, 1986).

Several of the more commonly-known programmes require extensive training and teacher experience. To learn about Feuerstein's Instrumental Enrichment, for example, a teacher must attend a lengthy programme at one of a small number of sites around the world – most training is undertaken in Israel. Other programme developers are keen to provide training where interest is shown but there is little opportunity for those to trial the newly acquired practices during training or to gain support from the developers once training has been completed. Regardless of their apparent potential, in most cases, the application of new cognitive education approaches is short-lived. This is especially true when:

- difficulties are encountered in applying fairly complex technologies (which add to the curriculum and have only a tenuous link to academic activities);
- student achievement gains are not forthcoming within a short period of time (many require long-term instruction to consolidate students' strategic and metastrategic behaviour); and
- there is little system-based encouragement for teachers to persist.

Perhaps the most serious pedagogical problem with many of the current programmes is their inflexibility in their application to classroom or individual learning settings. While many writers state their adherence to the principle of student involvement in the teaching and learning process, the overwhelming majority of programmes are teacher-designed, prescribed, and monitored approaches which limit student responsibility for learning. As such, they fail to account for individual differences in learning style. Under these conditions it is not surprising that students may not be motivated to adopt strategies or skills which seem incompatible with their needs.

One further point to consider when analysing the merits of any educational intervention is the degree to which it accommodates the interactions that take place between the learner and the programme, and the effect that this has on learning outcomes. This notion has been called the 'aptitude by treatment interaction' (or ATI) which accounts for numerous research findings which have shown that one instructional method, or 'treatment', may work well for some students and not for others because of variations in students' skills and abilities (that is, their aptitudes). If the treatment is changed, so might be students' levels of performance (Cronbach and Snow, 1977).

Few strategy-based training approaches have specifically addressed ATIs. Many researchers decide which strategies are needed for a specific skill and go about the process of teaching students how to use them. Of course, central to many approaches has been the desire to involve students actively in the teaching and learning process. This is certainly important in any programme; however, the weakness of many contemporary educational interventions is their failure to release both teacher and student from a relatively rigid instructional framework, in which teaching the strategy is the teacher's responsibility, and learning its application remains the student's.

Many programmes simply focus upon training one or a number of strategies which apply to a specific task. The implication is of a hierarchy of strategies, and Figure 3.2 graphically represents this notion. At the base of the triangle are those strategies which may apply to specific skills (e.g., a look–cover–write–check strategy for spelling). Toward the top may be found general strategies that are content non-specific and relate to awareness-raising and progress-monitoring (e.g., a self-talk strategy) which could apply in a variety of learning or problem-solving situations.

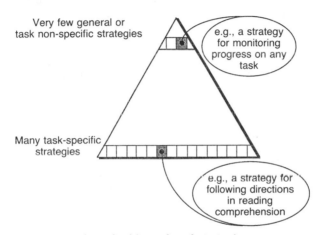

Figure 3.2 A representation of a hierarchy of strategies

It would seem logical to teach specific strategies which can be applied to specific skills or tasks, and general strategies which will enable students to monitor and amend their performance according to their success. Indeed, a number of cognitive education approaches adopt this principle. How students come to learn the range of strategies will depend upon the effectiveness of the programme and the ability of the teacher or trainer to ensure that the student understands and uses the strategies broadly and appropriately.

It makes sense, as many of the strategy training researchers in the early 1980s argued, to train specific strategies and metacognitive strategies in tandem. Some researchers have argued that students will recognize the generality of strategies as they become automatic users of them. Peat *et al.* (1989) make this point when they say: 'This process of extending and adapting strategies to new applications is designed to facilitate the modification and/or extension of the strategy taught in Phase 1, since most strategies can not be exactly duplicated as they are applied in varied settings, with different materials and with differing assignment requirement' (p. 99). They go on to say that a strategy would take on a very different form when compared to the original application. The difficulty that students encounter, however, is recognizing *when* and *in what situations* a strategy is applicable. Specific strategies do not lend themselves well to generalization because they are precisely that, specific strategies.

WHY PROCESS-BASED INSTRUCTION WAS DEVELOPED

PBI moves the focus of instruction away from the teaching of strategies *per se*. Strategy training, by itself, does not provide students with the link between the event in which learning takes place and the application of that learning in other contexts (Ashman and Conway, 1989). PBI was developed to:

- integrate learning processes and curriculum content;
- increase student participation in the teaching–learning process;
- link the four factors that affect successful learning outcomes (student, content, setting, teacher);
- teaching learning strategies that are applicable across content areas; and
- establish – or re-establish – a history of student learning success.

Practically everything we do throughout our lives involves problem-solving and planning and, hence, these two concepts are central to the PBI teaching–learning model and to the points made immediately above. We now turn our attention to a discussion of these concepts.

PROBLEM-SOLVING AND PLANNING

Learning how to learn about tasks and solve problems is one of the fundamental objectives of education, although it is rare for children to receive systematic instruction. Certainly, classroom instruction involves learning about tasks and how to perform them, what procedures are necessary for completing those tasks, and how and when to apply the procedures efficiently in it. However, most of the teaching and learning experiences are knowledge- or content-based, rather than process-based. Moreover, educators and researchers have used a (metaphoric) research microscope to examine learning in the context of the classroom, without considering how children learn a multitude of skills and knowledge outside school time. It is our belief that there are general learning and problem-solving procedures which can apply equally to the classroom and the less structured educational world of the child. It is toward these general concepts that we now turn our attention.

Problems and problem-solving skills allow us to deal with the many situations which challenge us each day. Problem-solving is the cognitive activity which turns thoughts into actions – changing an existing undesirable situation into one that is preferred. Many of the hundreds of problems we confront each day have many common elements (Bransford, *et al.*, 1986). Each situation requires us to make decisions (even if it is to make no decision), to formulate a plan of attack either deliberately or unconsciously, to undertake a set of actions, and to monitor our performance so that we know that we have achieved the goal.

Problem-solving is a complex activity which makes considerable demands on our cognitive skills. The successful and efficient resolution of the most basic or the most complex of problems, however, requires the premeditated use of essentially the same resources. This suggests that problem-solving is more conscious than unconscious, requiring continuous learning and adaptation.

Teaching problem-solving skills

There are two issues to be considered here: what to teach, and how it should be taught (see Burns and Lash, 1986, for more detail in this area). On the surface, the process appears to be quite simple. Teaching problem-solving would involve:

- how to derive maximum information from the problem being addressed;
- how to formulate a suitable strategy for its solution;
- how to enact the strategy; and
- how to monitor performance until the goal is achieved.

However, this can be said much more easily than it can be achieved. Let us examine the what and how components of problem-solving.

What to teach about problem-solving, and how

There has been some debate about whether there is a single set (or small number) of problem-solving elements that can be applied to a large number of tasks, or whether problem-solving simply means having very specific knowledge that is relevant to a particular situation. We have argued for the first option, suggesting that there are general competencies that are involved in the problem-solving process regardless of the nature or the context in which problem-solving takes place (Ashman and Conway, 1989). This set of competencies and processes is shown in Table 3.1.

In some cases, students can be given specific instruction on what must be done to solve a problem, while in others, general directions may be all that is needed to start the process. Doyle (1983), for instance, described two approaches. The first, direct instruction, refers to the use of explicit directions which involve a sequence of events or activities which seems to

Table 3.1 A list of problem-solving competencies and processes

What to teach	
Competencies	*Processes*
Knowledge needed to complete the task	How to organize knowledge so that it can apply to many problem-solving situations
Strategies and metastrategies which underlie successful performance	How to evaluate the problem itself; for example, looking for ambiguities in the instructions
Recognition of relationships and rules within the problem	How to use problem-solving procedures; that is, to apply systematically steps to search, scan, organize, set goals plan, and monitor
An understanding of systematic, problem-solving methods	How to gain and evaluate feedback on progress

be best suited for novice learners and students with learning problems. The second, indirect instruction, involves teaching higher-level cognitive processes to students who then discover appropriate problem-solving procedures and their application to other tasks. This approach seems more appropriate for older students who have well-established basic skills and knowledge bases.

There have also been several proposals concerning how problem-solving skills should be taught. Most writers have concentrated on describing procedures which relate to a small number of well-defined problems. For example, Derry, Hawkes, and Tsai (1987) outlined a set of procedures for improving deficient arithmetic skills, using an approach that included many of the points listed in Table 3.1. Others have been concerned with problem-solving procedures that may be applied to a range of cognitive activities. Fredericksen (1984), for example, listed a number of points that prompt the learner to structure the activity – these are shown in Table 3.2.

A simplification of this problem-solving sequence was suggested by Bransford *et al.* (1986) in the form of an easily-learned mnemonic, IDEAL.

Table 3.2 Generalizable problem-solving procedures

How to teach problem-solving skills

1	Verbalize the problem;
2	Get the complete picture without being concerned about the details;
3	Withhold judgement until all relevant information has been gathered;
4	Simplify the problem using words, diagrams, symbols or equations;
5	Try changing the way the problem is presented;
6	Make up questions and vary the form of the question;
7	Remain flexible in approach and challenge the assumption being made;
8	Try working backwards;
9	Work toward sub-goals that are part solutions; and
10	Use analogies and metaphors.

I	Identify
D	Define
E	Explore
A	Act
L	Look.

Identify refers to the recognition that a problem exists. For example, novice chess players may not perceive that they are only two moves away from being in checkmate. Students who are excellent readers will easily recognize that a passage contains incomplete or inconsistent information. *Define* means analyse what the problem is. Some ineffective problem-solvers do not consider the nature of the problem and, thus, are unable to identify a suitable strategy. *Explore* refers to the collection of information about the problem and its sources. This is the strategy selection phase of problem-solving, during which various options are considered, depending upon the type and nature of the task. *Act* relates to the tackling of the problem using the available resources, and *Look* refers to the monitoring of progress. This final procedure is used by successful problem-solvers to amend their activity when they encounter blockages. Some students, such as those with an intellectual disability, tend to be inflexible and do not adapt their activity to suit the demands of the task (see, for example, Gerber, 1983).

As will be clear from the points made above, successful problem-solving appears to involve the systematic application of a sequence of activities and thoughts – what was defined as a *plan* in Chapter 1. Planning, therefore, is a fundamental and essential component of all problem-solving behaviour, both inside and outside of the classroom. You will recall that planning is the process by which we put together a set of steps or a sequence of activities (a plan) that we believe will lead to success on a task. There will be times when we need a specific strategy; at other times, we will need to link both specific and general strategies to achieve the objective. To be successful in a task, we must not treat plans as fixed action sets. As we move toward a solution, it may be necessary to change the plan to take into account new information or blockages which are encountered.

THE NATURE OF PLANNING

Planning and problem-solving are closely related concepts. We can view planning as a continuous process that occurs in the brain. It allows us to integrate the stimulation that is occurring in various areas of the brain – which may originate outside of the person, such as sounds or visual information – to form thought patterns and thought sequences. Problem-solving can be viewed as the expression of planning – what we see occurring – when automatic responses (or reflexes) are insufficient.

Planning is important for all of us because it is intimately related to learning – some writers have even gone so far as to suggest that planning is learning (Hammond, 1990). Planning has direct links to the teaching–learning process, because of our need to organize information in a way which will allow us to:

- pay attention to what is to be learned;
- understand the relationship between the information being presented and what we already know;
- understand how we learn;
- control the rate and quality of learning; and
- be aware that learning has taken place (this is how we defined learning earlier in this chapter).

In other words, to learn effectively the student must deal with the incoming information in an organized and systematic way. As important as this is for a student to learn, to teach effectively as well, an instructor must present information in a systematic and organized fashion. Thus, planning must play a part in both teaching and learning.

The psychological concept of planning

Planning is not a new idea. There have been many reports of human activity relating to planning, in the psychology literature which dates back to the mid-1800s (see, for example, Harlow, 1848; Luria, 1973, 1980). In cognitive psychology, planning has been studied since the mid-1940s and tests of foresight and planning ability were included in the US Military Printed Classification Tests which were used as screening devices for aircrew recruits (Berger, Guilford, and Christensen, 1957).

Researchers have described planning as a fundamental part of the human organizational system (Miller, Galanter, and Pribram, 1960). While there has been much theorizing about planning,[7] several researchers have studied the practical use of plans in everyday life. For example, Byrne (1979, 1981) asked adults to think aloud in two studies: when organizing a series of dinner parties and when decorating a home. He analysed the spoken records of his subjects while they worked through the problem of deciding upon menus and ingredients for specific recipes, or of deciding the colours and furnishings for several rooms in a house. He suggested that imagery plays a major part in the planning process, by allowing people to form and evaluate decision-making procedures when working on the tasks. By executing plans mentally, we construct, test, and refine actions when real-world trials might be inappropriate – think, for example, what you might say and do if you had the Queen to your home for dinner.

A similar conclusion was reported by Dixon (1987). He examined the mental plans people make for carrying out written directions. He proposed that directions help to construct a hierarchy of mental plans. The top level of the hierarchy is a general, high-level description of the action to be performed (for example, 'Go to bed!') and the lower levels of the hierarchy specify the component actions to be undertaken in detail ('Turn off the TV, clean your teeth, put on your pyjamas . . .', and so on). Each element in the hierarchy contains ways of carrying out the steps. Dixon argued that for efficient planning, information relevant to the top level of the planning hierarchy should be given at the start of the directions (for example, at the beginning of a sentence or passage) and that information relevant to the lower levels of planning can be provided as required.

Finally, personality theory has been brought into the study of plans and planning. Kreitler and Kreitler (1986), for example, suggested that some people recognize certain cues more readily than others when those cues have special importance to them. A person who is disposed toward emotional responses will notice affective cues faster, solve problems containing emotional information faster, and have a richer network of affective associations than another who is not the emotional type.

A plan hierarchy

It would come as no surprise to any parent that, even at a very early age, children learn to link together actions to achieve goals. Problem-solving and planning are evident in the way in which youngsters can unfasten so-called child-proof locks, manage their parents' behaviour to win another hour of games or TV before they must go to bed, or solve a construction problem with their building blocks.

While young children may not recognize – or be able to explain to an adult – that they are creating and amending plans to achieve their objectives, they are nevertheless absorbed with planning. They can grasp the distinction between mental constructs (e.g., lunchtime) and physical entities (food) and have an understanding of the relationship between mental activities (e.g., wanting to open a cupboard) and actions (e.g., playing with the lock – see Cantor and Spiker, 1979; Wellman, 1990). The question is, how do children develop a sophisticated understanding of planning and plans as they grow older? Iran-Nejad (1990) suggested that learning complex information is not achieved simply through the enlargement of one's knowledge, but the 'creative *reconceptualization* of internal knowledge' (p. 586). This idea is reflected in De Lisi's (1990) view of the development of the planning process, in which he suggests that there is a change in the child's understanding of two plan features. The first is an awareness of the concept of a plan – embodying the notion of goals – and that certain actions are required to achieve the objective according to the circumstances. This is called the representational component of the planning process. The second constituent is the organizing or directing aspect of plans, called the functional component. For young children, plans are purely functional. They involve goal-directed behaviour, but there is no conscious recognition of the actions that are necessary to achieve the goal. With age, the representational component of plans becomes prominent, thus directing the functional component until the action sequence for a specific task becomes routine. In other words, children learn first how to perform a task before they comprehend what they are doing and why.[8]

De Lisi claimed that there is a dynamic relationship between the functional and representational components of plans. The relationship changes as children develop intellectually and as they alternate between novice and expert on various skills. This changing relationship between components has implications for educators. It suggests a need to vary task demands and to consider complementary approaches to problem-solving, depending upon the nature of the task and the knowledge and insights which are required by the student to perform it successfully. In other words, teachers must be sensitive to the aptitude by treatment interactions during the teaching and learning process.

Four forms of plan can be identified. We have called them undifferentiated, differentiated, strategic and projective plans. (Other writers have used slightly different labels.) This classification is based upon the goal and the context in which plans are generated.

Undifferentiated plans   These are those which are not consciously developed. Goal-directed behaviour and the recognition of the success or failure in achieving the goal may be apparent, but the person performs the task without an awareness of the need for a plan. Problem-solving is governed by good fortune or coincidence, rather than design. To the question, 'Why are you doing that?', a young child or an adult might answer 'I don't know, it just seemed like a good idea'. Some examples of undifferentiated plans might include a driver's habitual shoulder-check before changing lanes or a young child's persistent attempts to tie a shoe lace.

Differentiated plans   These are those in which there is a recognition of the need for a plan and a conscious attempt is made to develop a plan for a specific task. Differentiated plans are typically made when the person is confronted by a new or novel task, or when the knowledge needed to deal with the situation is not well understood. Some outside assistance may be needed to organize and refine the plan so that it is relevant to the task or context. The individual can articulate the goal and the steps within the plan, but may not be proficient in changing the plan to suit the changing demands of the task as progress toward the objective occurs. The boys described in Box 3.3 were engaged in a game that involved controlling the flow of water running down a slope which had been saturated by a sprinkler. Their behaviour is a good example of the use of differentiated plans, as they were able to articulate a plan for controlling the flow of water before they began to construct a canal and dam system. Some other examples of differentiated plans might include a student's plan for preparing a project on rain forests or an adult planning the landscaping of the back garden.

Box 3.3 An example of a differentiated plan

A sprinkler had saturated a wooded sloping area on a preschool property. The water had been trickling down the surface of the slope when it was discovered by four boys. The discovery seemed to be made worthwhile by the enjoyment they experienced running through the sprinkler, until one called to the others: 'Let's dam it up'. They stopped and watched the flowing water for a short time and each, independently, went to different places and began to create ditches across the slope through the leaf mulch and the soft earth beneath it. Water quickly filled the shallow channels and began to overflow. They chattered to one another about their progress as they worked to contain the flow of the water, then one boy cut across the channel created by another, which was about to overflow. The water divided.

They had soon criss-crossed the slope with channels, when one said, 'We need a dam', and went down the slope to a depression in the ground and began to form the wall of a dam. Two of the boys joined him in the excavation while the fourth 'battled' with the relentless flow by diverting water from one canal to another above the dam. By the time the three had scraped away a sizeable hole and built the wall, the other boy had constructed two main canals which drew water off the criss-crossed ditches and diverted it toward the sides of the dam.

'Let's build another one there!' one of the boys called, pointing to another shallow gully in the slope of the hill. The three were off quickly to the new excavation site while the fourth boy watched the first dam fill and begin to breach the wall.

The sprinkler continued to rain down its water; deep gutters were cut where shallow ditches had once existed in the slope. The fourth boy began patching the wall of the dam, but seeing this was futile by quick reference to the volume of water entering through the two canals, moved up the hill and began to extend the gutters toward the second dam.

It was not long before the second dam was completed and receiving water. All four boys stood back and watched as the water attacked their work. The canal system and the dams were working, but could not contain the gathering flood. They watched, soaked to the ankles, as the water cut each of the dam walls and continue its run down the slope.

The teacher called them in for juice. Ten minutes after they had started their construction, they ran down toward the play room.

To the observer, the boys' behaviour was systematic. They had begun by watching the flow of the water and had made clear decisions about how they could contain the run-off. Their attempts to control the flow of water were considered, acted upon, evaluated, and their plans amended accordingly. None of the boys were particularly communicative about what had to be done but all, from time to time, commented that they needed to contain the flow and, clearly, they had a mutual plan of attack and series of objectives.

Strategic plans   These are those which exemplify an obvious recognition of the goal, the need for a deliberate planning activity, and the contemplation of potential obstacles which may affect the achievement of the goal. The person is aware of the value of the planning process, the steps involved, and the relationship between the plan and goal-achievement. Enactment of the plan is flexible, permitting changes to the sequence as progress is made. Examples of strategic plans might include a football team's efforts to develop winning tactics for a game or an adult's scheme for ensuring that a forthcoming vacation will be a relaxing one.

Projective plans   These are speculative and hypothetical. The person undertakes the planning process on the understanding that the plan may never be enacted, or even needed. There is a recognition of the importance of a plan. The steps in the process can be articulated and decisions made about the need for alternative actions if events or circumstances change. Some examples of projective plans might include a child's consideration of what actions need to be taken if confronted by a stranger on the way home from school, or an adult's reflection on career options following redundancy or winning the pools.

While these four plan types reflect increased levels of planning sophistication, this does not mean that speculative planning is necessarily better or more desirable than the use of an undifferentiated plan. Each form has a place in learning and problem-solving. In the classroom, it is important for teachers to recognize the role each plan form may play in developing students' understanding of how learning and problem-solving occurs, and for them to encourage and support students' use of undifferentiated, differentiated, strategic and projective plans.

SUMMARY

In this chapter the discussion dealt with the nature of learning and a number of information processing concepts which allow us to describe how learning and problem-solving occurs. A number of cognitive education programmes were outlined, but these and many others tend to have limited application because of their narrow conceptual base. We then described a general process – planning – which appears to have a very clear application to the plethora of learning and problem-solving situations that occur across our lives. We have used this process as the foundation of Process-Based Instruction.

We believe that children who have the opportunity to learn about the process of planning in a methodical way, and have the chance to use and adapt plans, will become more independent in their learning and problem-solving endeavours. Furthermore, the classroom and the curriculum is the ideal context in which to introduce the planning process to children. In the next chapter, we begin to describe Process-Based Instruction as a model based upon these premises.

Chapter 4

An overview of the PBI model

In Chapters 2 and 3, you read about a number of factors that influence student performance in the classroom and about the importance of focusing on the interaction of these factors to aid teaching and learning. In this chapter we begin to outline the PBI model and its role in the teaching–learning process. In Chapters 5 and 6, we expand on these issues in a way which should enable teachers to introduce PBI into their own classroom or learning environments.

In this chapter the discussion focuses upon:

- an overview the PBI model;
- a definition of plans and planning in PBI terms;
- an outline of the characteristics of PBI plans and how they can be presented; and
- an explanation of the differences between PBI plans and other plan forms.

Before beginning, there are two terms that need to be defined – PBI plan and PBI model.

The PBI plan is a sequence of thoughts and actions that lead to the successful completion of the task.

The PBI model is based on the development of planning skills using PBI plans, first on a specific topic, then later through the broad application of plans to related topics and to diverse curriculum areas. Ultimately, plan development, use and adaptation is incorporated into the student's repertoire of learning strategies, and the teacher's repertoire of instructional strategies.

An explanation of each term is provided later in the chapter.

The teaching, learning and context factors to which we referred in Chapter 2 do not operate in isolation. They interact to influence what we teach and how we teach on a daily, or even hourly, basis. The teaching method used in any particular class will depend upon the importance assigned to each of these factors (or a combination of them) by the teacher. For example, in a class of low-achieving children a teacher may choose to be more directive, choose not to set a textbook because it is too difficult, and try to teach content in the morning, when the students are more responsive. In other circumstances, where there is a mandatory curriculum, some teachers may use a concrete, hands-on-materials approach, or even one which employs a discovery method.

Regardless of the approach or strategy used by the teacher, there will always be a number of students in every class who learn readily, and there will be some who do not. The important question to consider is whether there are correct combinations of teaching, learning and context factors which can maximize learning for each child.

As we mentioned in Chapter 1, PBI was developed as both a curriculum model and an instructional method. PBI is aimed at maximizing the positive impact of the four classroom teaching and learning factors (learner, content, setting, teacher). In other words, the PBI model will work in an extremely broad range of teaching and learning setting.

THE PBI MODEL

Many teachers will recall from their pre-service training programmes that learning is a complex process which involves linking new knowledge with information already held in memory. How we establish these links has always been a major challenge.[1] As classroom practitioners, teachers will no doubt have seen many parallels between student success on academic tasks and the varied ways in which both information and learning processes are conveyed to them. If teachers have worked at several grade levels, they may also have recognized how the mosaic of knowledge is formed, piece by piece, as children grow and develop.

You will recall from Chapter 3 that planning is a developmentally-based concept (moving from the use of undifferentiated to projective plans). The PBI model cultivates students' expanding knowledge of planning and the development, use and adaptation of plans within the framework of the curriculum. As such, it is a model of teaching, and learning.

The PBI model is a four-phase process which encompasses both the learning of specific skills and information, and the learning of general planning and monitoring procedures that apply in most, if not all, learning contexts. In each of these four phases, three teaching–learning strategies are employed (orientation, acquisition and application) to ensure that new information and/or skills are assimilated by learners into their existing knowledge bases. The model provides freedom for teachers to personalize the incorporation of planning into their own and their students' teaching and learning strategies, thus maximizing aptitude by treatment interactions (to which reference was made in Chapter 3).

The purpose of the four phases of the PBI model are outlined in Table 4.1. You will see that the planning process applies both to specific curriculum topics or exercises and to general learning (e.g., academic or non-academic activities). To engage the planning process, teachers and students develop, use and adapt plans to suit their own classroom circumstances.

Table 4.1 The four teaching–learning phases of the PBI model

Phase	Application of the planning process
Introduction	specific curriculum tasks
Establishment	curriculum tasks that have similar teaching–learning demands
Consolidation	tasks within a specific curriculum area or across curricula
Incorporation	learning in general

The phases in PBI are expressed diagrammatically in Figure 4.1.

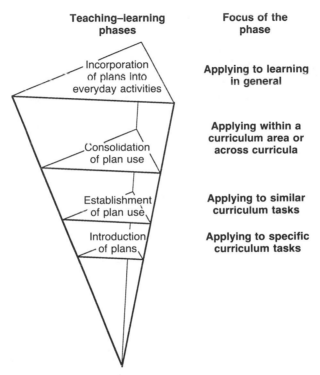

Figure 4.1 The teaching–learning phases, and their foci, involved in PBI

Each phase can be viewed as a section taken across an inverted triangular pyramid. The position of the phase (moving from the point base upwards) implies an expanding range of curriculum areas in which planning may be applied, depending upon the skills that students have acquired. We can think of the volume of the pyramid below any section as the knowledge base upon which PBI plans and planning are applied. The 'focus of the phase' indicates the expanding range of curriculum tasks to which students' new planning skills can be applied.

The rate at which teachers and students progress through the phases will depend upon the age and ability of the students and the instructional style of the teacher. We will discuss this in detail in Chapter 5.

PHASES OF THE PBI MODEL

Prior to introducing the PBI model, it is important to ensure that students are aware of what a plan is and how it can assist them in learning. The aim of this orientation exercise is to make students aware of the importance of plans for successful task completion and to provide motivation for the formal introduction to plans in the following phase. The best way to achieve this is by relating the concepts of plans and planning to the students' own lives. Using examples from everyday life is a very effective way of bridging the gap between undifferentiated (largely unconscious) and differentiated (process-oriented) plans, especially for young or primary school-aged children. Making children aware of the sequence and purpose of goal-directed activity will help them recognize the nature of the planning process. It will also remind them of the importance of plans as part of their home, school and social life, not only for themselves but for teachers, parents and other students. A variety of resources can act as a vehicle for discussion. Those which follow are but a few of a nearly unlimited supply:

- stories that feature planning behaviour (most books have a planning component which is found in the theme or plot);
- the teacher's plan for the daily programme;
- practical activities, such as preparing for a class excursion or fund-raising for the school;
- students may talk about their own plans, their families plans for holidays, sporting team plans for winning games, or plans they make with friends; and
- cartoon sequences (see Box 6.1, for example, on page 97).

For older students and adults who already know about planning and already form strategic and projective plans (e.g., studying for an exam, what to do with a lottery or pools win respectively), the orientation may involve no more than a few sentences. For example, the teacher may say, 'Planning is a pretty important part of completing activities successfully. We're going to use the idea of plans to help us with this problem. Here's how we can do it.' Older students may still enjoy discussing many of the activities listed immediately above.

Introduction

This phase, located nearest the point base of the pyramid, will provide the initial contact that students have with PBI if the teacher decides to introduce planning and plan use initially at the level of specific curriculum tasks.[2] The teacher may orient the students to plans and planning and follow this orientation with an exercise in which plans are used to consolidate the new skill or procedure.

The main focus of the phase is to provide students with their first formal experience of a PBI plan for a specific curriculum task. Students may be introduced to plans through:

- teacher-prepared plans;
- plans prepared jointly by the teacher and students, either before or after attempting the task; and
- student plans prepared individually or through a small group process, before or after attempting the task.

Some teachers prefer to introduce plans via a curriculum task that has recently been completed.[3] This allows students to see how the plan applies to a process which has a known outcome. When beginning PBI, it is often more effective to apply plans in one curriculum area, rather than across a number of subjects. The teacher and students may then concentrate on the development of functional and workable plans, without the confusion associated with changing content. It is most important that the first attempt at using a plan is successful and that students and teacher are satisfied with the experience in order to maintain enthusiasm for later plan use.

Establishment

Once students have become familiar with, and competent in, the use of the plans for specific curriculum tasks, it is important that they see the application of plans to a range of situations within the same curriculum area. At the primary level, for example, an initial plan for two column addition as a numeration exercise should be applicable to related tasks such as oral problems, written problems, measurement and space, both in classroom exercises and in applied settings. At the secondary level, a plan for reviewing a novel for an English assignment can be made applicable to another genre.

The crucial feature of the establishment phase is to ensure that the teacher and students do not become locked into the collection of specific plans for specific curriculum topics. If this were to occur students would need to recall a large number of individual plans each time a new task was presented. Students (or indeed, the teacher) must not become reliant on any one plan type.

Consolidation

The consolidation phase allows students and teachers to see that plans have a broader role in learning and problem-solving than simply the application to a specific curriculum task taught in class. Students are encouraged to identify tasks in other curriculum areas where a plan will assist in achieving the goal. Many teachers have reported that students readily apply plans to other subject areas, some in rather unexpected contexts. A class of adolescent students with mild intellectual disabilities, for example, were introduced to PBI by their home room teacher in reading and mathematics. They identified recipes and science experiments taught by other teachers as types of plans. Adults may recognize that recipes are not quite the same as plans, although there are strong similarities.[4]

As students become familiar with the use of plans in one curriculum area, they consolidate this by learning how plans can be abbreviated to make them of more general use – having few steps – or how they can be linked with other plans if a task involves a two- (or more) stage procedure. Both abbreviated and blended plans generally have steps that are more meta-cognitive in nature than those contained in single-purpose plans.

Incorporation

Once a student has a clear understanding of the use of PBI plans for a number of applications, they become more adept at making judgements about what actions or decisions are needed to deal with situations they encounter. They draw on their past planning experiences and on their knowledge of planning outcomes to guide their behaviour.[5] Incorporation, therefore, reflects three student competencies:

1 knowledge of how to develop, use and adapt both specific and general plans according to the circumstances;
2 an understanding of the constellation of learning and problem events that are appropriate at their particular developmental level; and
3 an ability to anticipate where planning success or failure may occur.

Learning which occurs within the instructional phases is also mediated by PBI plans – general organizational devices which can be applied to a wide range of curriculum and extra-curricular activities.

> The goal of PBI is to enable each student to become an independent learner and problem-solver with planning skills characterized by the three competencies outlined immediately above.

Within each phase, there is a cycle of teaching–learning strategies. In Figure 4.2 we show the cycle applying to the phase nearest the point base of the pyramid, 'Introduction of plans'. The same cycle (orientation, acquisition, application) would appear in each of the other phases.

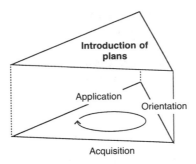

Figure 4.2 A graphic representation of the teaching–learning strategy cycle within the 'Introduction of plans' phase

The labels are nearly self-descriptive. 'Orientation' refers to the raising of learner awareness of the planning process within that phase. In the introduction phase, for example, this may involve a brief discussion with students about the need for a systematic approach when dealing with a specific mathematics topic. 'Acquisition' refers to the development, use and adaptation of a plan for a specified task (e.g., a plan for multiplication of terms in an algebraic equation). 'Application' refers to the appropriate (and successful) use of the plan in an activity or exercise based upon the topic (e.g., applying the plan to solve algebraic equations).

PBI PLANS

Planning is the conceptual foundation of the PBI model and the PBI plan is the agent of change that facilitates the development of planning ability. When beginning PBI, some students and teachers may think that using plans is all that PBI entails. This is not altogether surprising, because making and using plans is perhaps the one skill to which most attention is directed during in-service training. The reason why plans attract this attention is simple: getting plan development and plan use correct is critical for movement through the PBI phases. For the rest of this chapter, we concentrate solely on PBI plans, putting aside for the time being the developmental nature of the planning process.

The word 'plan' as it is used in the everyday sense is quite different to the PBI concept of a plan. From time to time, nearly everyone will make a plan: for the holidays, a shopping excursion, or to complete jobs around the home. Such plans allow us to identify a goal and have some general ideas about how it may be achieved. However, they rarely contain specific details of how to proceed, are almost never written down, and can seldom be followed by another person (even by a spouse who may, ostensibly, be working on the same plan).

Plans such as those made in the home serve an important purpose – they provide a framework to allow people to think through future actions. They work well if the task is a familiar one or if the person's planning skills are well-developed. Consider, however, how you might go about building a garden shed from raw materials, cooking a complex dish like Lobster Américaine, or constructing a balsa-wood model aeroplane for your children. For projects like these, there is a need for a sequence of written instructions, with perhaps some visual cues. The important difference between, for example, planning weekend activities and building a garden shed is the need, in the latter case, for a blueprint to assist in achieving the goal. These situations and their demands have close parallels to classroom activities.

For circumstances in which students have good planning skills or when an assigned task is straightforward, there may be no need for a plan. Other situations might call for a plan when the students do not have the knowledge, motivation or organization skills to complete the task, either unassisted or even with teacher assistance. In school, as at home, there will always be tasks that can be completed unassisted, those that can be completed with the assistance of a plan, and still others that are beyond a person's current abilities, regardless of the amount of assistance provided. When a plan is needed it should be a PBI plan, and we now turn to consider the characteristics of PBI plans.

Characteristics

Earlier in this chapter a definition of PBI plans was presented.

> PBI plans are sequences of thoughts and actions that lead to the successful completion of the task.

PBI plans conform to a number of general guidelines:

1 They must provide a starting point. Students must know where to start and how to start the task before them. Without a clear beginning, students may sit waiting for the teacher to tell them what to do, or engage in task-avoidance behaviour such as pencil sharpening – rather than attempting the task unaided.
2 PBI plans must follow a sequence, with each step in the plan leading to the next. Many people will have seen the toy called a Slinky, which is a spring that will tumble down a staircase mechanically, one step at a time, when it has been set on its journey. In the same way, the learner must move through the PBI plan from one step to the next, unaided.

3 PBI plans must contain thinking (i.e., metacognitive) steps which require the student to make judgements or decisions about the actions taking place. These are part of the monitoring and verifying process that students undertake as they progress toward successful completion of the task. Without a monitoring component, a plan is merely a set of directions for which no confirmation of progress is required.

4 PBI plans must lead to the successful completion of the task.

5 PBI plans are designed for use by students or groups of students without the need for direct teacher assistance. Hence, plans have value not only as a teaching device but also as an independent learning strategy, allowing the teacher a degree of flexibility to work on a one-to-one basis with some students while others may use a plan to work independently.

These five points can be operationalized into the four key plan components: cuing, acting, monitoring, verifying (see Table 4.2). All plans contain the four components, but there may be loops within plans. For example, a plan may contain two cuing steps, followed by three acting steps, a monitoring step, another acting step and finally a verifying step. In some plans a step may have dual functions (e.g., acting *and* monitoring).

Table 4.2 The key components of a PBI plan

Component	Target
Cuing	Where to start?
	How to start?
Acting	What is the essential sequence of actions needed?
Monitoring	Is the plan working as expected?
Verifying	Has the task been completed correctly?
	Do I finish or go back and try again?

All PBI plans must contain these four components but plans may not necessarily have only four steps. There are commonly loops within plans.

Making PBI plans

Plans can be prepared by the teacher, students, or teacher and students together. How the initial plan is prepared will depend on whether the teacher wishes to introduce students to plans by providing an example (one that is teacher-made) or by having students develop a plan by themselves or in collaboration with others (a student/teacher-made plan).

Teacher-made plans   An example of a teacher-made plan for use with a class of ten-year-olds is shown in Box 4.1. Notice that it contains a series of sentences that are sequenced and include a cuing step (1), an acting step (2), a monitoring step (3), possibly another acting step (4), a second monitoring step (5), and, finally, a verifying step (6).

It is important to realize that teacher-made plans use teacher language. Being prepared by a teacher, they may not conform to the language structure commonly used by students in the class.[6] Hence, teachers must develop prototype plans that are used as models only. Students must then be encouraged to make modifications which make the purpose and process clear to them.

> The translation of prototype plans into student plans (that are re-written by the students in their own language) is one characteristic of PBI which sets it apart from other cognitive education approaches.[7]

In this way, students will gain a sense of ownership of the plan as they record it in their own words.

Box 4.1 A plan for writing a paragraph

> 1 What is the paragraph to be about?
> 2 Write sentences.
> 3 Have you said what you want?
> 4 Revise sentences if needed.
> 5 Does the paragraph make sense?
> 6 Share your work
>
> Note: This is a teacher-made plan that
> needs to be adapted for student
> use by changing the wording into
> student-oriented language

Student/teacher-made plans   To avoid the need to translate teacher plans into student language, many teachers prefer to involve students in the preparation of plans right from the start. In Box 4.2 is an example of a plan developed jointly by a classroom teacher and her class of six-year-old students. Notice again that the plan contains the cuing (1), acting (2 and 3), monitoring (4) and verifying (5) components. It is worthwhile noting here that step 3, 'punctuate', was added to give special emphasis to the need for children to check that their sentences have been punctuated correctly.

This plan differs from the one shown in Box 4.1, in that it contains both pictorial (rebus) and written steps. It is not written in sentence form but has single words to cue each step. Both the teacher and students contributed ideas to the discussion about writing sentences which resulted in a plan that used pictorial steps only. Later, the class added word steps to help consolidate ideas that they would be using later in the year. The use of visual

Box 4.2 A jointly-prepared PBI plan for writing and punctuating a sentence

and word steps in one plan provides a link for action and meaning and assists students to connect the ideas.

The plans in Boxes 4.1 and 4.2 were developed as a result of teacher dissatisfaction with the approach recommended in a curriculum document. Hence, the plans met the teachers' needs in the written language arts area. In one case the teacher chose to provide the students with a prototype, while the other teacher chose to involve the class in the development of the plan.

There are no prescribed methods for making and using plans. Teachers are free to integrate plan development into their regular teaching strategies in any way that supports their personal teaching style. They must decide, however, if a plan is needed for a particular classroom activity and, if so, how the planning process can best be incorporated into the lesson or learning experience. The familiarity of the students with PBI, their level of academic achievement and the teacher's desired level of control over classroom routines will affect the choice. A range of options is given in Table 4.3. Because of the flexibility of the approach, an item in any column can be crossed with one in any other – in other words, there are 3 × 3 × 4 possible combinations.

Presenting plans

There is no predetermined presentation format for PBI plans and, in fact, there is no single correct PBI plan for a curriculum task or activity. Teachers may use any metaphor or motivating technique to encourage students to develop and use PBI plans and to convey the message.

Table 4.3 A summary of the ways in which plans can be made

	PBI plans can be	
prepared by	*when*	*in which form*
teacher	prior to attempting the task	oral
students – individually, in small groups, or at the whole class level	when attempting the task	written
jointly by the teacher and the students – individually, in small groups, or at the whole class level	following the completion of the task	rebus, photographs or pictures
		a combination of the above

Note: cross an item in one column with items in other columns

Sometimes people see plans as being similar to computer programs (see Box 4.3), in that they require the user to follow a particular sequence of steps to achieve success. The difference, however, is that PBI plans can be modified to meet changing student needs, whereas a programming sequence remains fixed. The plan shown in Box 4.3 was prepared by a class of 11-year-old students soon after they had completed a computer literacy course. It occurred to the students that a plan was similar to a computer flow diagram and they prepared the plan to reflect that form.

This plan, like the others shown earlier, might be appropriate for the establishment or consolidation phases, as it has more general application than to a specific activity. It will work for addition with carrying to the tens column *and* for addition without carrying. This is an important distinction, between task-specific plans, which in this case work only for addition with carrying, *or* addition without carrying, and task-general plans which work effectively across a number of domains.

Task-general plans could be used for revision or, in the example being used here, for helping students decide when they need to carry.

For students at the pre-school level, early grades, or for those who have an intellectual disability, the plan may be presented entirely in pictorial format (see Box 4.4, and Box 5.7 on page 85). Alternatively, the plan may consist of photographs that are taken while the students are attempting the task, which can then be sequenced to form the plan. Photographs have the advantage of representing the events accurately – a significant consideration for students at an early developmental level. One warning must be sounded here. Students must understand the *meaning* of the pictures or the

Box 4.3 A plan for two-column addition

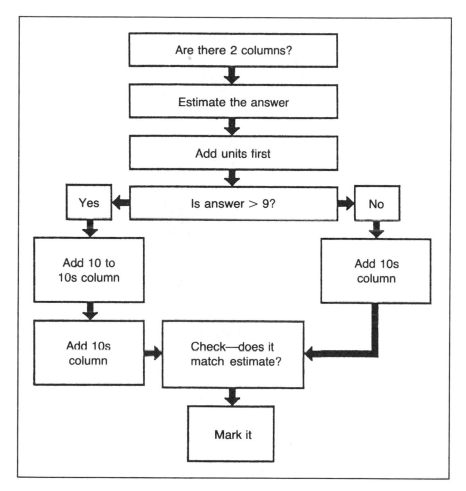

photographs and be able to perform the actions or thoughts required if they are to move from step to step unaided through the plan.

In mathematics, it may be appropriate to include an example of the operation to accompany each step of the plan. Box 4.5 shows an example of subtraction which demonstrates how the plan can be applied to each step of the mathematical operation. Students must realize that the example is not part of the plan *per se*. If the plan is written on cardboard and covered with a plastic coating, any number of examples could be written on the plastic coating to demonstrate how to use the plan – perhaps a new example each time it is used – thus avoiding the impression that the plan works for one example only.

Box 4.4 Example of a plan using drawings – 'Our trip to the zoo'

5.  Write
Sentences

Add, change

6.  Read
Check

st ⇨
Finish

- Add, change
- Punctuate
  'I'. ! ? " "
- Spelling
- Does it make sense?

7.

Share
the story

Box 4.5 A plan for subtracting with trading

1. Read	$\begin{array}{r} 34\,- \\ 18 \end{array}$
2. Estimate	
3. Look	$\begin{array}{r} 34\,- \\ 18 \end{array}$
4. Trade	$\begin{array}{r} {}^{2}\cancel{3}{}^{1}4\,- \\ 18 \end{array}$
5. Write	$\begin{array}{r} 34\,- \\ 18 \\ \hline 16 \end{array}$
6. Check	$\checkmark$ or $\times$

The number of steps in a plan

There are five or six steps in the sample plans shown in the boxes above. Some students will need plans which have more steps, while others may require less. It is better to err on the side of too many than too few steps initially (within reason), thus giving students the opportunity to reduce the number of steps before recording the final (and personalized) plan. This has the advantage of involving the students directly in the planning process at an early stage, thereby increasing the likelihood of their ownership of the plan. A brief anecdote will exemplify this point:

> Some time ago, a senior secondary history teacher prepared a prototype plan for writing history essays, which contained 14 steps. When she presented the plan to the class, the student decided very quickly that many steps were superfluous and, during a brief class discussion, they eliminated half of them. The working plan – which they ultimately accepted as the class plan – contained only seven steps. The teacher had accomplished two important goals: she had provided the opportunity for the students to be involved in the decision-making process, and students had accepted ownership of the planning process.

Occasionally, the number of steps in a plan are insufficient for students to use it effectively. Earlier in this chapter we used a metaphor – the Slinky spring toy tumbling down a staircase – to describe the manner in which a learner progresses from step to step through the plan. Extending the metaphor, if there is a tread missing in the staircase, or if the treads are too wide or the risers too high, the toy will stop on one tread, or fall out of control. In much the same way, if the plan has missing steps or if one or more steps are too large or too difficult, students' learning or problem-solving behaviour will falter and they will be unable to complete the task without teacher intervention.

It is not unusual to encounter situations in which the PBI plan is inappropriate for one or a number of students in any class. The plan must be revised at the group or individual level, to ensure that the necessary steps are included to allow each student to achieve success on the curriculum activity.

In summary, PBI plans are:

- instructional tools to aid teaching and learning;
- developed to meet specific teaching and learning needs;
- action and thinking sequences which lead to successful task completion;
- made and changed as the circumstances demand;
- irrelevant when the student has consolidated their understanding of the task or activity; and
- always related to student judgements and understanding of the process.

Some fine distinctions

Not all tasks require an understanding of process. For example, a young girl learning her home address and telephone number does not need to think through the process of how the details are learned. She must simply be able to recall the information when required. There are other teaching tools – such as rules and directions – that are used in the classroom and which are sometimes confused with PBI plans. It is important to distinguish between them at this point to avoid later misunderstandings.

Rules   These are sets of prescribed actions that apply to a task. When students learn a rule for combining elements in chemistry (based upon the valence of an element), or a rule for spelling ('i before e except after c'), it is not necessity for them to understand why the rule works – although we often hope that they do. In other words, the rule can be applied without comprehension.

Rules apply to tasks and not to learners. Here is another example:

In English, whenever you have a consonent-vowel-consonent word, the addition of 'e' at the end of the word changes the middle vowel to sound its alphabetic name.

Rules are fixed and are only applied when the student recognizes their relevance. They are:

- applicable to a specific task only;
- unchangeable, otherwise they will not work;
- used whenever the relevant task is to be performed;
- action-based procedures;
- applicable without student comprehension of the process; and
- outcome-oriented.

Directions   These are most often confused with PBI plans. Directions, such as cooking recipes, are usually actions which are to be performed in a prescribed sequence, although in some cases the order is of little consequence. PBI plans and directions are similar in that an optimum number of steps is required for task completion. Unlike PBI plans, the person following a set of directions may not be required to make judgements or to understand the process being enacted. In summary, directions are:

- performance-oriented;
- developed to achieve a consistent performance or to establish a routine;
- a list of activities or actions;
- most often a prescribed action sequences;

Box 4.6 A young student's 'plan' for cleaning the dog

Box 4.7 An example of a teacher-made plan and a PBI plan for an arithmetic task

I was given £63 for my birthday. I spent £15 on drinks for my friends. I put £25 into my bank account. How much do I still have left of my birthday money?

Directions	*Plan*
1 Add up how much was used	1 Read the problem
2 Write down how much there was at the start	2 How much did I start with?
3 Take away what was used	3 Calculate the total amount used
4 Write the answer	4 Calculate – what's left?
5 Check the answer	5 Check the answer

- redundant when the skill is attained or when learning has occurred; and
- applicable without student understanding of their purpose.

When students are learning to make and use PBI plans in the classroom, many begin by making sets of directions as they tend to place emphasis on the actions involved in completing a task rather than on the decisions that are needed to maintain progress. Plans made by young children exemplify this tendency. The so-called plan in Box 4.6, for example, is really a set of directions. Box 4.7 shows the difference between preparing a set of directions and a plan for a curriculum task. Notice that the plan requires thinking and monitoring.

SUMMARY

Rules, directions and PBI plans all have a place inside and outside the classroom. We make the distinction between them solely to indicate that they are relevant to teaching and learning at different times and in different circumstances. While student comprehension of why rules or directions apply to a task or a curriculum activity is always desirable, it is not an essential feature of their use. This becomes obvious when students misapply rules or when they follow a set of directions which will not achieve their objective – they fail most often when students with learning problems are involved.

In this chapter, we have presented the main principles of PBI. At this point, you should be able to:

- outline the phases of the PBI model and describe the importance of moving through them;
- name and describe the three teaching–learning strategies and their purposes;
- define a PBI plan and its four components;
- list the types and forms of PBI plans;

- describe how PBI plans are developed; and
- distinguish between plans, rules and directions.

Before moving on to the next chapter, you might take a few minutes to test yourself on the six points listed above. Check back in the chapter if you are not clear on any of the details. In the following chapter, we shall explore how to begin using PBI in a systematic way and learn how to prepare a PBI plan.

Chapter 5

Preparing to use PBI

In the previous chapter we outlined the phases and the teaching–learning strategies that constitute the PBI model. The objective of PBI is to develop and consolidate a range of planning skills that are hierarchical in terms of their generality. The nature of the task or the problem being confronted dictates the form of plan that is needed. In Chapter 4, the distinction was also made between PBI plans, rules and sets of directions. Once again, we stress that each of these tools has a role to play in effective teaching and learning, but the most important for PBI is the PBI plan.

In this chapter we continue the description of PBI and how it can be applied to the classroom. This includes:

- how to adapt the examples of PBI plans given in the book to the realities of teaching in your situation; and
- how to prepare for initial PBI-focused lessons, including personal practice in plan-making.

Occasionally we receive feedback from teachers suggesting that the examples of PBI plans we have used during in-service programmes are irrelevant to their personal teaching situation. Some are secondary teachers who, while understanding the purpose of the primary-level plans we have used, are not able to translate the concepts into a secondary-level teaching context. The same difficulties are experienced by primary teachers who are unable to generalize from secondary-level plans.

In this chapter we provide many examples of PBI plans. While it might be possible to provide models of plans for all subject areas at all grade levels, within the limitations imposed here it is unrealistic. As a consequence of this, we urge you to look beyond the actual *content* of the plans, especially if they are not directly relevant to your class, and focus on the *principles* which the plans exemplify. In this way you can personalize this book for your own teaching situation. While librarians may fall back in horror at the suggestion, you might pencil in your own versions of plans in the book, if this will help you clarify their development, use and amendment, and the PBI process itself.

For this chapter to be of maximum value, you should be familiar with the content covered in earlier chapters, especially Chapter 4.

PBI is based upon the belief that training in planning and metacognitive skills must be integrated into the usual teaching programme. Before you begin PBI, it is important to consider:

- the students you have in your class;
- the curriculum you are teaching;
- the strategies that you have found effective; and
- your philosophy of teaching.

This may sound like a mammoth task, but most teachers will already have a good idea of how these factors affect their teaching, although they may not have formalized it. Thinking over these four points before beginning to develop PBI plans will help overcome many of the operational problems some teachers experience in the early stages of its introduction into the classroom.

STUDENT CONSIDERATIONS

If you are teaching in an early childhood/pre-school setting or in an elementary/primary school you will spend most of your teaching day with the same group of students. You will gain a good understanding of their performance levels across curriculum areas and can readily identify those students whom you think might benefit most from learning within a PBI context. If you teach in a secondary or high school, you will have a number of classes of different age and ability levels. Consequently, it is unlikely that you will have an overview of each student's ability across curriculum areas, and your PBI programme will focus exclusively on your subject specialization.

Plan to introduce PBI at the whole class level. Occasionally, a teacher in a mixed ability class will restrict the use of plans to those students who are having learning difficulties and the results may be disappointing. Strategies used only with weaker students become labelled as 'for dumb kids only' and neither regular students nor the weaker students will use them. PBI is designed for all students – bright, average, and weak – and all teaching and learning situations.

Most teachers are quick to recognize students' aptitude and can readily assign students in their classes to groups according to ability. While there are a number of ways to group children depending upon the learning context, allocating students to work groups based upon ability remains a common procedure when learning involves complex thinking processes. Obviously, it would be excessive to group students by aptitude for every classroom activity. Being aware of students' knowledge and skills is important because it will sensitize the teacher to the range of responses students may make to plans when they are presented as part of a class lesson or learning activity.

Elsewhere, we suggested three categories into which students might be

Table 5.1 Categories of learners for any specific curriculum task

Category A	These are students who are able to complete the specific task without teacher assistance or the use of a PBI plan
Category B	These are students who can complete the specific task with teacher assistance and/or the use of a PBI plan
Category C	These are students who are unable to complete the specific task and who should be attempting a lower-level task within the task analysis.

placed – Category A, B, and C level learners (Ashman and Conway, 1989). This is based upon students' capabilities in respect of a specific task within the skill task analysis (see Table 5.1).

Autonomous learners on a specific task (Category A) have the opportunity to use their skills in planning to move immediately to higher levels of planning and, perhaps, to the development of speculative and projective plans. This group of students may also take the plan being used by peers in the Category B group in the class and work on reducing the number of steps or altering it for more difficult examples. Category A students may also provide tutoring assistance to the Category B group in the class. Some care needs to be taken in using this technique, however, as Category A students may be academically able but might have modest planning skills. Furthermore, some teachers may be less than enthusiastic about peer-tutoring methods.[1]

Students who require guidance in learning (Category B) are the main targets of PBI, as they are ready to attempt the task but require teacher input to learn. As teachers tend to focus their attention on this group of students in most class teaching situations, plans can easily be accommodated in most classrooms.

For dependent learners (Category C), the current teaching task is too difficult and success is an unrealistic expectation (you will recall Scott's predicament described in Box 2.2 on pages 22–3). Ideally, they should attempt an easier task, perhaps one which is a prerequisite for the current activity. In many classrooms, however, they are required to attempt the same task as the average and above-average students, often with lamentable outcomes.

Developing and amending a PBI class plan is one way of providing an opportunity for all students to achieve success on the task or topic. If all students participate in the discussion and amendment of the plan and its suitability for their own learning needs, the plan should be appropriate for those in both Categories B *and* C. However, it is often the case that the less able students do not participate fully in planning sessions, particularly when they are uncomfortable about asking for clarification, and when they do not fully understand the development and adaptation of plans. One way of involving all students is to use small mixed ability groups in initial discussions to develop reciprocal learning skills (e.g., children using their own words rather than the teacher's). If the task is well beyond the capabilities of some students, even the best PBI plan will not lead to a successful outcome. An appropriate alternative is to set those students an easier task, while the others in the class work on the original activity.

CURRICULUM AND TEACHING STRATEGIES

For many teachers, the curriculum provides the major driving force in determining teaching content. Many schools – particularly secondary schools – have prescribed curriculum topics to be covered within the year, leaving little time for teachers to assist students who need more guidance, or to extend the autonomous students. So prescriptive are some contexts that the method of content presentation is also predetermined. In contrast, learning that is based upon processes of understanding – rather than curriculum content – can be flexibly applied to any learning context. This was a point raised by Daniels (1990), and it is a strength of Process-Based Instruction.

Teachers have used PBI successfully across a wide variety of curriculum areas, including mathematics, language arts (reading, spelling, writing), social science, science, craft, vocational and self-help skills. It has also been used in conjunction with organizational skills such as research and project planning, essay writing, classroom routines and group work, and as a framework for behaviour management programmes that focus on student responsibility for behaviour (this is considered further in Chapter 8).

Primary school teachers often begin using PBI in mathematics or language arts because many of the common teaching strategies in these curriculum areas can be easily adapted to fit a PBI plan format (for example, the 'look, cover, write, check' strategy for spelling, or the 'brain-storm, draft, conference, edit, publish' strategy for writing). Secondary teachers tend to start with plans for written activities, as essays and reports are common to most, if not all, curriculum areas. Using plans where they are linked to everyday classroom teaching practices is an excellent way to begin PBI.

Teachers tend to avoid using PBI plans in areas in which the instructional procedures are not clearly prescribed, because they are not sure how to conceive or develop a plan. A common way in which teachers have dealt with this issue is to present the problem to their class. Students are often very responsive during brain-storming sessions and may contribute many innovative ideas which will lead readily to plan development and use.

Preparing a lesson which incorporates a plan is no more difficult than preparing one which does not, if the teacher is resourceful. The next few pages exemplify how PBI can be applied at various grades and ability levels in a number of curriculum areas.

Language arts/English

The language arts (English foundation subject) curriculum provides many opportunities for teachers to use PBI plans, particularly where the emphasis is on students accepting responsibility for writing. Many teachers are unable to supervise each student directly during a writing exercise or lesson. For bright students, the brain-storm, draft, . . . teaching–learning sequence can be a PBI plan as it would provide them with the metacognitive steps needed for a successful outcome. For some students, however, the brain-storm, draft, conference, edit, publish sequence does not make a lot of sense. Consequently they devote considerable energy to avoiding contact with the teacher and, hence, are extremely unproductive. For them the sequence is not a plan; the steps are not clearly understood, as they convey insufficient information. Plans may be needed at each level in the writing process – for a sentence, paragraph, story and an essay. Examples of the first levels of this hierarchy were shown in the previous chapter. These PBI plans turn the writing process into a meaningful activity for their particular level of ability.

The writing process (or process writing) is part of a 'top-down' approach to language arts/English in which reading, writing and spelling are integrated. Through guided exposure to literature and writing, students learn specific skills. A PBI plan can also be appropriate when a skill-specific or 'bottom-up' approach to reading is used. In this case a plan could assist in teaching a phonic decoding skill, as shown in Box 5.1 (in which the actual plan and an explanation of the plan are given, although students would see only the pictorial plan). This plan was prepared by the class and teacher and can be applied to a number of phonic groupings, making it very versatile.

Box 5.1 A PBI plan for sounding words

Explanation	Actual plan
1 Look at the word	①
2 Find the chunk	② paid
3 Sound the chunk	③ ai
4 Sound out the beginning, chunk and ending	④ p..ai..d
5 Say the word	⑤ paid

Mathematics

The highly task-analysed nature of the mathematics curriculum at the primary and secondary school levels permits easy identification of skills which may then be introduced, applied or revised using a PBI plan. An example from the previous chapter (of addition with and without carrying – Box 4.3 on page 67) would be appropriate when teaching discrimination between addition with, and without, carrying to the tens column. Providing an example written beside plan steps (Box 4.5 on page 70) is a practical way of assisting students to use the plan, although the example should be changed each time the plan is used, to ensure that students do not gain the impression that the plan works for one case only.

Clearly, plans can also be prepared in other areas of the primary mathematics curriculum for topics such as money, space and measurement. These applications might extend the use of a plan developed for a basic operation, as shown above. Any plan that is applicable only to numeration has limited value.

Plans can also be prepared easily for aspects of the secondary mathematics curriculum, including geometry, algebra, calculus and trigonometry. Box 5.2 illustrates a plan developed cooperatively by a group of 14-year-old secondary students and their teacher in a remedial mathematics class. This example demonstrates the importance of preparing a generalized plan that has application beyond the area of one specific shape (such as a rectangle). Note the four components of the plan: cuing (1, 2 and 3), acting (4 and 6), monitoring (5), and verifying (7).

Box 5.2 Plan for calculating area

```
1 Name the shape
2 Know the size
3 Know the rule
4 Write the rule down
5 Check the rule
6 Work it out
7 Check the answer
```

Science

In the primary school grades, many teachers have used PBI plans to underscore the importance of the systematic study of the physical world. Teachers and students have used plans for studying the effects of growing conditions, electrical circuit experiments, and the preparation and testing of chemical solutions, to name just a few activities. Box 5.3 shows an unusual plan developed by a Grade 2 teacher and her class for learning about

Box 5.3 A PBI plan for a description of an Australian animal

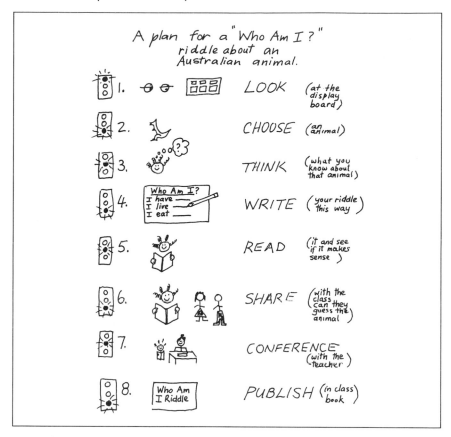

A plan for a "Who Am I ?" riddle about an Australian animal.

1. LOOK (at the display board)

2. CHOOSE (an animal)

3. THINK (what you know about that animal)

4. WRITE (your riddle this way)

5. READ (it and see if it makes sense)

6. SHARE (with the class can they guess the animal)

7. CONFERENCE (with the teacher)

8. PUBLISH (in class book)

Australian animals. A feature of the plan is the use of traffic lights as guides to cuing (red), acting (green), and monitoring and verifying (yellow) steps. At the secondary school level, students have used plans for environmental science, for the preparation of chemical compounds, and for experiments on electricity and friction, to name just a few areas.

Social and vocational skills

Plans are useful for teaching social and vocational skills to students with an intellectual disability, as these students typically are poor planners and can benefit greatly from the structure provided within a plan to assist them to learn. While students with serious learning problems can be slow to understand the concept of a PBI plan, once established, they can use and readily apply the planning process when they are confronted with difficult, new or novel tasks:

> One group of 14-year-old students attending a special class in a large high school were introduced to PBI by their home room teacher. After six months of working with her for 20 periods a week, the students had become accustomed to plans and the planning process, had learned to make plans as a group, and how to ensure that all members of the (small) class were able to use them. To several teachers' surprise, the students began to use plans independently with favourable result when attending other classes in which PBI was not used.

Plans for students with an intellectual disability often employ pictures or photographs. An example of a plan used by two teachers working with a group of children with moderate intellectual disability is shown in Box 5.4.

Box 5.4 A PBI plan for sandwich-making

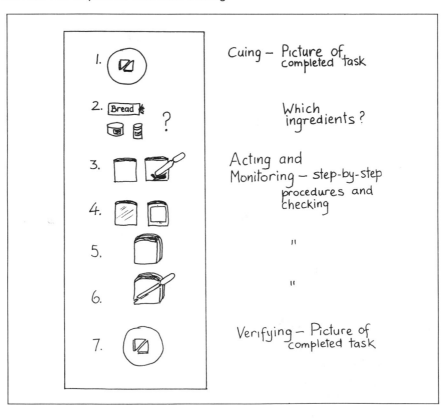

Notice that the cuing step includes a picture of the completed task. This provides a model of the appropriate outcome for the students.

Organizational skills

For many teachers at the secondary level, the lack of appropriate preparation of students engaged in projects or major essays is a source of some consternation. Plans are often used by PBI teachers to assist their students to develop and apply research and study skills which lead to completion of their assignment.

A teacher-made prototype plan for preparing a secondary curriculum essay is shown in Box 5.5. It was made by a teacher during a PBI in-service workshop and might have more steps than necessary for some students. However, this plan could be readily adapted for primary school projects or for tertiary essays, and students could amend or edit the plan to suit their needs. The teacher has emphasized the cuing steps (1 to 3) to ensure that students adopt the desired orientation to the essay.

Box 5.5 A PBI plan for preparing an essay

```
 1  Read the question – think
 2  Underline the important parts of the question
 3  Reread the question
 4  Library search for references
 5  Read references and make notes
 6  Plan outline – introduction
                 – body
                 – conclusions
 7  Write first draft
 8  Have I answered the question?
 9  Make changes if necessary
10  Write up references
11  Final check OK?
12  Submit on time
```

The plan in Box 5.5 may not suit all students or teachers. In some cases, the plan would need to reflect the curriculum area taught and the desired essay format.

An organizational plan developed by a student in Grade 5 for completing her mathematics homework is shown in Box 5.6. This was the student's first attempt at writing an organizational plan, yet it contains all the components of a PBI plan and would easily be followed by other students.

Box 5.6 How to do homework

Think about what day it is
Make sure I know what to do

1 Collect all the things I will need:
      pencil
      eraser
      homework book
      calculator
2 If it is a sum, work it out then write it down
3 Check my answer on a calculator
   If it's wrong, rub it out and correct it
   Ask myself: 'Have I done it right?'
                'Is it my best?'
4 Get my parents to check it

Plans in the early school years

PBI has been used successfully in many pre-school, kindergarten and Grade 1 classes. From a developmental point of view, it is important to convey the message to these young children that the events which take place around them – and which include them – do not occur randomly. It is also important to develop an awareness of, and the need for, classroom routines and procedures.[2] Probably the most appropriate context in which plans can be used with very young children are those in which organizational skills are required. Frequently the main need at the early childhood level is for plans that focus on transition activities such as getting started, packing and unpacking materials, and putting equipment away. Box 5.7 shows a plan used by a pre-school teacher for putting shoes away in the locker after they are taken off. The final step in the plan is the pre-school teacher's way of having the students verify that they have not misplaced any of their property.

TEACHING STRATEGIES

As we mentioned in the last chapter, PBI plans can be used by teachers who adopt widely differing teaching approaches and methods. Those who prefer to work in a direct, teacher-controlled learning environment tend to develop their own, teacher-made plans initially to provide a model of the standards expected of students.

It is essential, however, that students are given the opportunity to amend the teacher's prototype plans to ensure understanding and student ownership of the plan.

Box 5.7 A PBI plan for putting shoes away

Explanation	Actual plan
1 Shoes off	
2 Think where they go	
3 Walk to the lockers	
4 Put shoes in locker	
5 Check lost property box	

Later, as students become accustomed to plan use and amendment, they should also be given the chance to develop plans themselves so that planning becomes part of their repertoire of skills, rather than simply remaining a teacher-based strategy.

Teachers who see their role as facilitators in the learning process may allow students to work with concrete materials to discover relationships and then assist them to develop a plan which reflects the discovery. This approach provides students with the opportunity to learn in a cooperative environment in which group dynamics change according to the social, ability, interest or group foci. When students work together, it is more likely that plans will reflect their language rather than the adult's, and more likely that plans will be understood by the students.

Group work is a very effective method of transferring some of the responsibility for teaching and learning to the students. When it is used for research and projects, students may work cooperatively to plan and complete an assigned task. Group work also provides a context in which reciprocal teaching skills can be developed to enhance learning and planning behaviour.[3] In reciprocal teaching, students take turns in the roles of teacher and student. This may facilitate and reinforce plan development and adaptation more effectively than would be the case in other learning settings in which instruction is provided in adult language.

Our description of PBI up to this point may seem to imply that it is a whole classroom strategy only. This is not the case. PBI has much to offer the generalist teacher, the subject specialist, the resource, support or remedial teacher, and consultants and administrators. Resource personnel who support classroom teachers, for example, are frequently called upon to assist failing students who are unable to use appropriate learning strategies. Poor strategy use may take many forms – rehearsal or sequencing difficulties, the use of unsystematic approaches to academic tasks, or investing less persistence and effort than is needed to complete a task. All these skills can be assisted by the development and use of appropriate plans, and the resource teacher can assist students to understand how to learn, rather than simply provide them with content.

Resource teachers and consultants can also affect the teaching–learning process in the classroom by encouraging teachers to incorporate metacognitive processes in their teaching. Along with school administrators, support staff often have a school-wide view of teaching and are in an excellent position to introduce and coordinate PBI across grades and throughout the school.

INCORPORATING PLANNING ACROSS GRADES

The impact of PBI across grades or the whole school will not be conspicuous in the first year of use. It will be more obvious in subsequent years when

Table 5.2 Planning goals across grades*

Developmental group	Planning goal
1	oral to rebus plans plans for daily activities stories to demonstrate plans planning excursions general plans for curriculum tasks and behaviour
2	oral/rebus to written plans plans for curriculum topics planning excursions general plans
3	written plans plans for curriculum topics plans across curriculum areas planning as a general skill student plans
4	blending and reducing plans general plans initiating planning in/out of the current curriculum peer instruction
5	plans within subject curriculum areas generalizing and evaluating plans plans for study plans as organization mechanisms

* *Note* that these goals are not intended to be followed rigidly – they are guidelines only, based upon interpretations of the planning literature

teachers have become accustomed to using plans, and when there is no need to emphasize PBI plans each time they present new skills and content. A whole-school approach to PBI provides the context in which learning strategies are presented developmentally in much the same way as content is taught as a developmental sequence. Table 5.2 may provide some markers for the development of planning skills across grades.

There is an implication here that the goals listed in Group 1 apply to developmentally younger students than those in Group 5. So, Group 1 might apply to pre-school and the beginning school years; Group 4 goals might be relevant at the end of primary or elementary school, while Group 5 may apply in junior high school. However, it is important to stress that the goals do not link directly to specific grades. The objectives that a teacher may establish for any group of students will depend upon:

- student abilities and skills;
- the instructional preferences of the teacher; and
- familiarity of both teacher and students with PBI procedures.

The important point to make here is that students have the opportunity to see plans operate in a variety of contexts, regardless of their age or ability. In other words, they experience each of the teaching learning phases which comprise the PBI model.

PBI AND INTEGRATION

Special education classrooms and resource rooms have low teacher–student ratios and focus on individualized programmes with some group work. Students are often closely supervised while attempting tasks and receive frequent feedback to maintain their progress. Many special class programmes, particularly those for students with intellectual disabilities, focus on the acquisition of academic, social, personal and vocational skills, rather than on the general curriculum of a regular classroom.

The focus is typically on skill acquisition at the expense of instruction that emphasizes an understanding of the process involved in using the skill. As a result, students who are having difficulty learning the skills are often unable to progress without the prompting or consistent reinforcement of the teacher or teacher's aide.

The focus of many social skill programmes prior to integration seemed to be the development of appropriate interpersonal skills for situations which may arise in the regular classroom. However, students preparing for integration need to develop not only appropriate social skills but also learning skills that will enable them to work independently or with minimal supervision within the mainstream classroom. Regular class teachers do not have the time – or in some cases the inclination – to work as intensively with integrated students as would have been the case in the special classroom.

Independence in learning is, therefore, an important prerequisite skill for mainstream classrooms. This can be assisted through the use of PBI plans which can focus on learning skills within both social and academic domains.

An integration teacher or resource teacher can support both the integrated student and the regular classroom teacher. The integration process can be accelerated by providing additional assistance to the student in planning skills through the use of PBI plans and by demonstrating the effectiveness of PBI to the class teacher, perhaps using a team teaching model. Providing integrated students with the 'coping' skills needed for the classroom is particularly important when they will be working on tasks or activities that are different to those of their mainstream classmates. The most effective preparation is for PBI to be introduced into the special and regular classes concurrently prior to integration, so that there is a supportive learning environment when students take their place in their new class.

Where PBI is being used in the regular class prior to integration, the class teacher may still need some assistance from the integration or resource/support teacher to support plan use when the integrated student is working at a different level to that of the rest of the class. In this case the class teacher may, on some occasions, teach the class using one level of plan while the support person works with the integrated student at another level. On other occasions, the support person may work with the class while the class teacher works on a one-to-one basis with the integrated student.

WHEN TO USE, AND WHEN NOT TO USE, A PLAN

Plans are not always the most appropriate way of introducing new content or of revising content. All teaching and learning strategies can lose their impact if they are the *only* strategy used.

> One Grade 6 teacher became very enthusiastic about PBI after attending an in-service programme, and set about incorporating plan development and use in his teaching programme. Plans were made for the school assembly, coming to the classroom, getting started, for spelling, mathematics, social studies, reading, library research, being cooperative, and doing homework, to name just a few applications.
>
> It took about a week of bombardment with the planning process before the students were thoroughly, and understandably, tired of plans. Cries of 'Not another plan!' and 'Can't we just do it our way?' became more and more frequent. After about two weeks, the teacher tempered his enthusiasm, used no plans for a month and then gradually reintroduced PBI plans for specific activities, achieving much greater success than he had in the first two weeks.

PBI plans are best used:

- when the teacher wants students to understand both the content *and* the process, rather than the content alone;
- when students are having difficulty with a previously taught task and need a plan to guide them through the task; and
- when the teacher is working with a student individually or with a small group while others are working on an exercise or activity for which they already have a PBI plan.

In each of these cases, a plan will enable students to remain on-task and productive, rather than having them wait for teacher assistance. There is still a need to teach the content to the students – the plan is simply the supporting instructional aid.

As we have indicated before, PBI is more than the presentation and use of a visible plan. It involves the systematic and explicit instruction and application of planning skills; hence it is critical to check students' familiarity with the planning process. This can be done in a number of ways – for example, by asking students to make a plan for a classroom exercise, or simply by allowing them to decide when a plan is needed. Those students who are familiar with the application of PBI plans can assess task demands and use their planning experience to formulate, trial and amend plans (if they are needed). Building the assessment of planning skills into usual evaluation practices will require little effort but it will allow the teacher to see whether planning strategies have been internalized or are triggered only by teacher instruction. Assessment of planning skills can produce valuable information which can be used to assist individual students who are having difficulty with plan development, use or adaptation.

ADAPTING PBI PLANS TO YOUR SITUATION

PBI will be a useful teaching and learning model, regardless of whether you work with individual students, small groups or whole classes or whether you prefer a direct instruction, data-based instruction or a teaching–learning approach which follows the aptitude-by-treatment interaction principle.[4]

The only approach that is inconsistent with PBI is one which dissuades student involvement in the teaching–learning process, requiring only rote production of the content.

Because every class and every teacher is different, we are philosophically opposed to prescriptive teaching methods that aim to make everyone fit into the same learning sequence. As you have seen already, there is no book of plans or specific formats for any curriculum area or grade. Each teacher, therefore, must understand how to make a PBI plan and how to apply it to their particular circumstances.

While the plans presented in the various chapters of this book cover a wide range of teaching situations, it is not possible to provide examples for all curriculum areas at all grade levels. If they are relevant, you will need to adapt the sample plans and their layouts to meet the curriculum and teaching requirements of your classroom and school.

Before introducing PBI into your classroom, resource room or other teaching–learning situation, you must be fully conversant with the concept of a PBI plan and be able to construct a plan yourself. Because there is no book of plans, teachers must develop or adapt plans to meet the needs of the educational situation in which they work. The remainder of this chapter, and indeed the remainder of the book, is designed to guide you through the preparation and introduction of plans into the classroom.

It was mentioned earlier that students frequently construct a set of directions rather than a PBI plan, before they learn the difference between them. Teachers also may prepare teaching plans or sets of directions, rather than student-oriented PBI plans during their first attempt. One of the easiest ways of avoiding this trap is to develop a teaching plan first and then translate it into a PBI plan.

A teacher's plan for making a plan (Box 5.8) may be of assistance. This PBI plan is designed to guide teachers who prefer to introduce a teacher-made plan in the first instance, rather than jointly developing one with students – although the general principles are important for all plan construction.

Box 5.8 A plan to make initial plans as a teacher

```
1  Is the task appropriate for the students (task analysis)?
2  What prerequisite skills should students have?
3  Make a teaching plan
4  Change the teaching plan into a student plan ('you will' becomes 'I will')
5  Simplify the wording in each step, perhaps to one word or a drawing
6  Change teacher language into student language
7  Ensure that the plan has cuing, acting, monitoring and verifying components
8  Review the plan to check that it achieves the task confirmed in step 1.
9  Present the plan as a prototype, allowing the students to alter it to
   meet their needs.
```

MAKING YOUR FIRST PLAN

It is now time to attempt your first PBI plan. As each reader will have a different background, different students and different educational respon-sibilities, we recommended that your first plan be at a teacher level, to avoid the need to translate the plan into one that is suitable for students.

As many teachers have studied at the tertiary level, a good starting place for practising plan development is to prepare a plan for writing a university-level essay. Assume that you are to write a plan to assist your colleagues with the task (i.e., to write an essay at university level). The final plan must allow your colleagues to use the plan unassisted to achieve a completed essay.

If you feel confident to continue with the preparation of the plan, use a photocopy of the plan format shown in the Appendix; when you have finished, return to this point in the book. Readers who would like assistance may simply continue reading this section.

Follow the plan in Box 5.8. Let's begin by asking three questions:

What is the goal?   To complete and submit a university-level essay.

What do the students know?   How to conduct a literature search and write an essay.

What should the students know after using the plan?   How to prepare a completed, researched and coherent essay that is submitted on time and which will achieve a good grade.

Having established what is to be taught and what the expected outcomes of the plan are, the development of the plan can commence. Read through the steps below and then reread the steps while attempting to prepare a plan of your own. We have left sufficient space on the right of the page, if it would help to make notes right here in the book. Alternatively, you might photocopy the blanks in the Appendix.

Step 1: Is it appropriate for the students (task analysis)?
We will assume that the topic of the essay is appropriate.

Step 2: What prerequisite skills should students have?
We will assume that the students know how to conduct a literature search, and understand the mechanics involved in writing essays. If this were not so, a prerequisite plan for literature searching or writing would be required.

Step 3: Make a teaching plan.
List all the steps that need to be undertaken. Don't worry if the list is not in the correct order or if it is excessively long at this stage.

Step 4: Change the teaching plan into a student plan.
Look for places where you have been instructive or directive (e.g., implying 'you will') and change the words into a form that is first person (e.g., implying 'I will').

Step 5: Simplify the wording of each step.
Reorganize the list. See if it contains steps that can be logically subsumed by other steps, and decide the format of the plan (e.g., words, sentences, computer flow diagram).

Step 6: Change teacher language into student language.
Simplify the language format – reduce to telegraphic writing if possible. (In this exercise, the words you use might well be quite suitable for a colleague, but this may not be the case if you were preparing a plan for a group of students who were developmentally young.)

Step 7: Ensure that the plan has the four components.
Check that you have cuing, acting, monitoring and verifying components. Remember that a step might

include cuing and acting
components, or acting and
monitoring components,
and so on. This is quite
appropriate, especially
when the task is a
conceptually difficult one.

Step 8: Review the plan.
Does the plan make sense,
and will it achieve its aim
using only prerequisite
knowledge. In this case, do
you expect other teachers
will be able to follow it?

**Step 9: Present the plan as a
prototype.**
You may like to show your
plan to a colleague and ask
if it should be modified in
any way. A high essay score
will be the verification!

Re-check that your plan satisfies the criteria in Table 5.3. If it does not,
make any changes before proceeding.

Now that you have had experience in preparing a plan on a task that is
at teacher-level, the next test is to prepare a plan at the student level.

Table 5.3 A short PBI plan checklist

1	Is the plan a sequence which will allow the student to progress from one step to the next?
2	Can the person complete the plan unassisted?
3	Does the plan require thoughts and actions, rather than simply being a set of directions?
4	Does the plan contain steps that can be identified as cuing, acting, monitoring or verifying steps (or a combination of these components)?*

* Sometimes it is not possible to say definitively if a step in the plan is a cuing or an acting
step, or an acting or monitoring step, or a monitoring or verifying step. Some steps may
suggest all of these processes. If you can't label the step because you can't decide which
component it represents, don't be concerned – you will already have satisfied this item in
the checklist.

Choose a curriculum task that you are about to teach or which you have taught recently. This may be in any area of the curriculum, or it may be an organizational plan relating to work skills or social skill management. Using the plan form in the Appendix, complete the three preparatory questions. Proceed through the steps discussed above to complete a plan. Remember that the plan has to be translated into student language and that the students must be able to follow your prototype without your assistance or prompting.

Once you have developed the plan, you may wish to show it to a colleague who teaches the same grade or the same students and ask this person to check it against the list in Table 5.3. Remember, the plan presented to the students does not have to be perfect. Checking by a colleague ensures that the teacher plan is a good model for students. After you have completed this exercise, you may choose to develop a number of plans for recent or current teaching topics across a number of areas of the curriculum, to develop your skills in plan construction and evaluation.

If you choose to develop plans jointly with your students rather than presenting your prototype to them as a model, you should still practise the development of plans, as outlined above. This will ensure that you become fully aware of the presentation and structure of plans, and that you can assist students to develop plans while modelling good planning skills.

SUMMARY

This chapter has dealt predominantly with PBI plans. It is suggested that plans be introduced first for specific tasks, to ensure that students gain success. Later their application can be expanded to other tasks within the same curriculum area, and finally, across curricula. We discussed alternative plan formats and the goal of having students take responsibility for the development of plans. Translating plans into student language, either directly through students' development of the plan or through translation of a teacher plan, was highlighted as one of the features of PBI which sets it apart from most other cognitive education approaches.

Finally, the chapter gave the reader an introduction to plan development through two hands-on experiences of preparing a teacher level plan for writing an essay and of preparing a plan for a task related to current teaching. The following chapters continue to elaborate on the implementation of PBI in your classroom.

Chapter 6

Starting PBI in the classroom

In this chapter we discuss the way in which PBI can be introduced into the classroom and will deal with the first two teaching–learning phases:

Introduction – which involves:

- orienting students to plans and planning;
- selecting the appropriate PBI instructional mode for your students;
- introducing the first PBI plan;
- applying the orientation, acquisition and application strategies to specific task plans; and
- integrating PBI more generally into your teaching practice.

Establishment – which involves:

- changing plans to accommodate new examples;
- recording and storing plans for future use;
- applying the orientation, acquisition and application strategies to plans within curriculum areas; and
- increasing student responsibility for plan development.

THE INTRODUCTION PHASE

The initial teaching–learning phase has two important parts:

- orientation to plans and planning prior to the first use of a PBI plan, and
- introduction of PBI plans to students within a curriculum area.

The relationship between the introduction phase and other phases in the model is shown diagrammatically in Figure 6.1. Plans are developed on a small number of curriculum topics to ensure that maximum attention is given to plan development, with minimum variation in curriculum content.

Orientation to plans and planning

For students to become efficient plan users, they must understand clearly the relevance of plans and planning to their daily lives and to the many

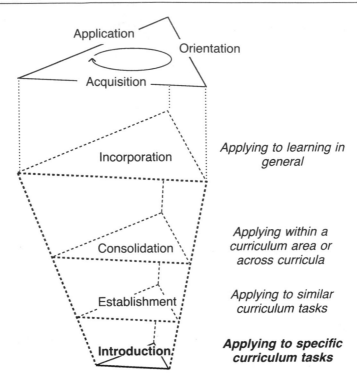

Figure 6.1 Relationship between the introduction and other phases of the PBI model

learning experiences they encounter. Initial discussions, stories and practical activities are important in demonstrating to students that plans and planning are part of their everyday lives. Here are a number of ways in which teachers have dealt with these concepts before introducing the first academically-oriented PBI plan.

Discussions   Class or group discussions are the most usual way that teachers at all grade levels draw students' attention to plan use and the planning process. These include individual and group planning experiences such as planning a school excursion, a fund-raising event or some classroom-based activity (e.g., a library session). Teachers can point to the many ways in which they plan their teaching day, including the preparation of materials, checking that the programme for the day is proceeding, and making alteration to the schedule in response to unexpected interruptions.

Stories   An alternative or supplement to discussions is the use of stories that feature planning. Most stories have an underlying planning component within the theme and discussions can centre on what would happen as a result of the plan, or what might happen if the plan does not succeed. Students can plan their own stories and, perhaps, include within them a series of alternative plans, depending on what they decide will happen at particular points in the story. This can be a very useful language arts lesson.

Visuals or story lines   The graphic shown in Box 6.1 has been widely used at the primary and secondary school level for orienting students to the idea that using a plan leads to success. Teachers have displayed the cartoon above the blackboard or have reproduced it for inclusion in students' workbooks. Students have been encouraged to consider why one boy was successful and the other was not, rather than being told by the teacher. In addition students should be encouraged to discuss other situations in which a plan may mean the difference between success and failure.

Practical activities   If the students are about to undertake a practical activity such as an excursion, or a school event such as a fête or sports day, planning can focus on preparations for the event. Be certain to introduce the concept of thinking and monitoring into the plan, to ensure that it is not simply a set of directions.

No time is set for the completion of the orientation section. Generally speaking, students who have had no exposure to plans and planning, or

Box 6.1 Which boy had a plan?

who are young or have severe learning problems, will take longer to understand the concepts than older or more capable students. If you have used a variety of examples and techniques to introduce plans and planning, you and the students should be ready to begin developing and using a PBI plan on a curriculum task. A checklist of the skills that should have been acquired by the students at the end of the orientation section of this phase is shown in Table 6.1.

Table 6.1 A checklist for orientation

1 Do the students understand the concept of plans?
2 Do the students understand the value of plans and the planning process?
3 Are students aware that plans can be used on curriculum tasks?
4 Are there any students who may not have grasped the concept? You may need to spend some time with these students individually to complete their orientation.

Acquisition and application – the first lesson

In the same way that you were introduced to plans in Chapters 4 and 5, your students will now be ready to learn how to develop plans. Before beginning, you need to decide two matters:

● the curriculum topic that you will use to introduce the plan; and
● the form that the plan will take.

It is best to introduce the first PBI plan to the whole class or group for ease of instruction. This avoids the problem of the plan being seen as a strategy which is to be used only by weak or bright students. It also provides a good model for all students on how to develop and amend plans to meet individual needs.

Topic   Once you have established which subject or area you will use, or which organizational skill you wish to teach, you must then decide whether to introduce the initial plan based on new, unfamiliar content, or whether a familiar topic that has been recently covered would be more appropriate. Using a new topic takes advantage of the novelty factor, which may be quite motivating for the students. If you decide to make the plan jointly with the students, this option will work very well.

If you choose to introduce a prototype to the students and then test whether it will work, it may be appropriate to select a topic with which the students are already familiar. This has the advantage of linking the plan to students' existing knowledge so that at the completion of the exercise they are able to verify that the plan works. It is important to remember that the topic chosen for the initial plan must not be beyond the capabilities of the students, as it is unlikely that they will perceive the value of the plan and may be suspicious of using them in the future.

Integrating plans into classroom activities   The differences between teacher-made and student-made plans was discussed in Chapter 4. Such a distinction might suggest that there are only two ways in which plans can be constructed. In fact there are many ways to integrate the planning process into classroom activities. Box 6.2 shows six alternatives, which have been called modes. Try Mode A (teacher-made plan) or Mode C (class, group, individual plan development following an activity) for the initial lesson.

A teacher-made plan provides a model which should guide the students through the task to achieve success and the model must demonstrate a combination of action and thinking steps. The teacher must always remember to encourage students to adapt the plan so that it is in student language, or in a form with which students are comfortable (e.g., pictures or rebus).

Student/teacher-made plans also have advantages. They will generally be constructed in student language from the outset and will give students the challenge of creating their first plan rather than gaining the information from the teacher. This approach to plan development will only work effectively if students have some skills in cooperative learning and information sharing. Although the plan is student/teacher developed, the teacher must enter the discussion with a clear idea of how the final plan may look, in order to guide students in plan development.

Box 6.2 Modes of introducing PBI plans to students

Mode A   Suitable when introducing a new topic without first establishing the task process, for example, using concrete materials in mathematics to teach addition, or providing an existing plan for a science experiment.

1 Teacher presents a PBI plan on a chart or on the blackboard.
2 Students follow the plan with or without help from the teacher.
3 Students copy the plan from the chart or blackboard in their own words.

Mode B   Suitable when introducing the planning concept to a group of students or when a plan is to be used for locating information in a specific topic.

1 Teacher gives the class the content to be learned in the form of a problem.
2 The class makes up a PBI plan to solve the problem.
3 Students trial the plan.
4 Students copy the class plan in their own words.

Mode C   Suitable when working with young students, or older students with a developmental disability, or in other situations in which the sequence of activities is important but students are not required to record the plan.

1 The teacher prepares a visual PBI plan using a series of pictures/rebus (that will be used later in Step 3) but the students are provided only with the task requirements verbally.
2 Students carry out the activity using concrete materials.
3 The class then develops a PBI plan by sequencing the teacher's pictures/rebus (students may not necessarily record the plan).

Mode D   Suitable when the aim is to have students understand the process of completing the task. There are many primary and secondary activities for which this mode is appropriate.

1 The teacher prepares a possible PBI student plan (i.e., without teacher language) but the students are provided only with the task requirements.
2 Students carry out the activity using concrete materials and develop a PBI plan individually or in groups.
3 Students record the plan in their own words.

Mode E   Suitable when it is important for students to think through the planning process themselves. Again, there are many activities at all developmental levels for which this mode is appropriate.

1 The teacher gives the class an oral PBI plan.
2 Students carry out the plan.
3 Students record the plan in their own words.

Mode F   Suitable when working with Category A students on a new topic, or any group of students once plans are incorporated into the teaching–learning process.

1 Individual or small groups of students are given the topic content.
2 Students develop a group plan or individual PBI plans.
3 Students trial either the group or their individual plan.
4 Students teach their plan to a small group or to the class.
5 Individual students record the plan in their own words.

The four components of a PBI plan   When developing the first (and, indeed, any) PBI plan it is essential to ensure that the plan contains steps which include cuing, acting, monitoring and verifying components. It is unnecessary to label steps as 'the cuing step', or 'the verifying step'. In fact, it is much better if these labels are stated implicitly rather than explicitly, as labelling may lead the students or teacher to identify one step for each of the four components and forget that plans have loops and combinations of the four components.

One of the more effective ways of developing a functional plan is to have the students develop a prototype plan first, and then for the teacher to suggest that the plan should have:

● a clear starting-point so that the person reading it knows how and where to start;
● acting steps with clear directions about what is to be done;

- thinking steps that check how the plan is going; and
- a final checking step (or steps) to make sure the task has been completed correctly.

Using codes for the four components is one way to ensure that each is included. One mathematics teacher, for example, incorporated shapes into her mathematics plan (see Box 6.3). The shapes assisted students in two ways: they helped them to remember the need to include all components in each plan, and they acted as a visual guide to the purpose of each step.

Box 6.3 Incorporating the four components within a visual plan

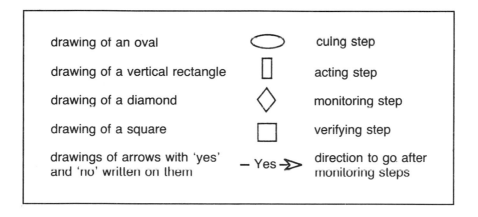

drawing of an oval	⬭	culng step
drawing of a vertical rectangle	▯	acting step
drawing of a diamond	◇	monitoring step
drawing of a square	▢	verifying step
drawings of arrows with 'yes' and 'no' written on them	– Yes ⇒	direction to go after monitoring steps

The first PBI plan

Having selected the topic and the way in which the plan will be integrated into the lesson (the presentation format), the teacher can proceed to develop and/or trial the first plan. Two approaches are discussed below (of the six modes described in Box 6.2). You should apply the presentation format that best meets your needs, but avoid using the same one each time a new plan is introduced.

A teacher-made plan   An example of a lesson sequence is shown in Table 6.2 below. This is only a guide, and must be adapted to meet each teaching situation. This approach requires considerable teacher input into the lesson to provide a prototype and to have students test it. You will note that student involvement occurs at the plan revision stage. As suggested earlier, this approach is perhaps best used for a task that has been covered in an earlier lesson, so that any complication due to new content is avoided.

Table 6.2 Using a teacher-made plan to introduce PBI plans

1 Teacher reminds students of earlier discussions on plans and planning.
2 Teacher explains the curriculum task to the students.
3 Teacher presents the prototype plan to class.
4 Teacher explains the steps of the plan, highlighting the four components of a plan.
5 Students attempt the task using the plan.
6 Teacher and students discuss the plan's effectiveness.
7 Teacher and students amend plan, ensuring that it will achieve the goal.
8 Students attempt another example using the revised plan.
9 Additional revisions are made, if necessary.
10 Students and teacher record amended plan.

A student/teacher-made plan   Having made a prototype plan for the task, the teacher guides the students through the development of the plan. A typical teaching sequence is shown in Table 6.3.

Table 6.3 Using a student–teacher plan to introduce PBI plans

1 Teacher reminds students of earlier discussions on plans and planning.
2 Teacher explains the curriculum task to the students.
3 Students attempt the task individually or in groups.
4 Students and teacher discuss the strategies used in completing the task.
5 Students and teacher develop a plan for attempting the task.
6 Teacher introduces the importance of the four components of a plan and discusses with students how these relate to the plan.
7 Students revise the plan, ensuring that it will achieve the goal.
8 Students attempt another example, to test the plan.
9 Students revise the plan, if needed.
10 Students and teacher record the amended plan.

The plans developed as a result of the initial lesson may be used in subsequent lessons or on alternative examples based on the same curriculum topic.

> It is important that students realize that planning is not a one-off event. It is a process that will help them to succeed in class and in other activities outside of the school.

An example of how one teacher involved her Grade 8 students to develop a student/teacher-made plan is illustrated below. The teacher was working with a group of 14-year-old students who were attending a remedial mathematics class in a large rural secondary school. The challenge was to find the area of a shape. Box 6.4 traces the development of the lesson and the final plan is given at the end.

Box 6.4 Developing a student/teacher-made plan for finding the area of a shape

Locating areas		Teacher asks students to locate the face of shapes in the room, including desks, books.
Looking at one shape		Teacher holds up square and asks students how they would calculate the area.
		Students discuss the need to know the length of sides and how to calculate area. Students and teacher begin to record plan on blackboard:
	Plan Step 1	Name the shape.
	Plan Step 2	Know the sides?
	Plan Step 3	Know the rule?
Calculating the area		Students identify the formula for area of a square as $A=s^2$ and calculate the area:
	Plan Step 4	Write the rule down.
	Plan Step 5	Work it out.
Monitoring		Teacher introduced monitoring into the plan by asking students how they would know whether the answer was correct. Students decided to add Step 6.
	Plan Step 6	Check the answer.
Class read out plan		
Teacher trial of plan		Teacher demonstrated application of the plan to a rectangular shape 7m × 4m.
Rechecking of plan		Students took turns reading the steps of the plan and enacting them on the blackboard.
		Students realized the need for additional monitoring step.
	Plan Step 4a	Check the rule.
Review of plan		Teacher and students reviewed the revised plan.
Preparation for lesson		Teacher alerted students that in the next lesson on the following day the plan would be used for calculating the area of other shapes and the plan could be further reviewed by the students before recording it in their books.

The final version of the plan was:
1 Name the shape.
2 Know the sides?
3 Know the rule?
4 Write the rule down.
5 Check the rule.
6 Work it out.
7 Check the answer.

The lesson described in Box 6.4 demonstrates the role of the teacher in assisting students to develop a plan. By providing practical activities at the beginning, she focused the students' attention on area as a measure of the size of the face of an object. She used concrete objects to reinforce the prior knowledge of area of a square. She reminded the students of the importance of verifying their answer rather than accepting that it was complete, and hence, correct. By asking the students to apply the plan to a rectangle, she tested the generality of the plan. By asking the students to work cooperatively through the plan, she triggered the need to include an additional monitoring step which was volunteered by two students, demonstrating that they had perceived the need for both acting and thinking steps. As a result the class produced a plan which was then used successfully to complete an exercise on area.

It is crucial that the plan should be successful in the initial lesson; however, it need not necessarily be perfect. It is also important that the planning process is enjoyable for the students, especially for those who have a history of failure. Table 6.4 provides a number of questions which will help streamline the plan development stage.

The introduction phase may take as little as one class period to complete, or as much as a year, depending upon the age and ability levels of the students. While task-specific plans characterize the introduction phase, it is important to remember that they can be used at any time when the need for such a plan arises.

Table 6.4 A checklist for the introduction phase

1 Do students understand how a plan is constructed?
2 Have students had the opportunity to be involved in developing plans?
3 Are students able to incorporate the four PBI components in their plans?
4 Have you provided students with the opportunity to translate plans into student language?
5 Have you consistently used plans on a specific curriculum task so that plans are no longer a novelty but are, instead, a learning strategy?
6 Are both the students and you ready to apply plans across similar tasks?

If the answers to the questions above are 'Yes', the students are ready to move on to the next phase of the model – establishment.

THE ESTABLISHMENT PHASE

This phase is designed to increase the generality of plan development, use and adaptation. Once again, the teaching–learning strategies (orientation, acquisition, application) are employed to demonstrate that plans may be used on a specific task, but they can also be adapted to suit others with similar curriculum demands. The PBI model (Figure 6.2) shows this broadening of plan application.

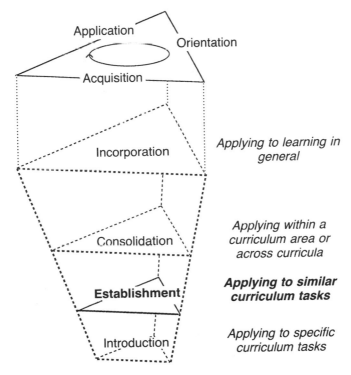

Figure 6.2 Relationship between the establishment and other phases in the PBI model

By the time the students have used a number of plans for specific curriculum topics, they will have developed a basic understanding of how PBI plans are made, used and adapted, although they will have limited experience in applying them. If plan use in the introduction phase is restricted to teacher-made plans, it is important now to allow students to prepare their own plans. This applies to students at all developmental stages.

The establishment phase operates at two levels. At the application level, it involves extending plan use from situations in which they apply to one task only, to those that involve alternate content for which the same skill is

Box 6.5 An outline of a lesson in which a PBI plan was developed for finding project information

1 **Ideas stage**	Teacher hands out books on animals to each student
	Discussion on skills of examining books • look at the book quickly • look at cover – title, picture • look at index • look at contents page • look at pictures
2 **Draft plan for finding specific information**	Step 1 Read title. Step 2 Look in the index. Step 3 Look at the contents page for a chapter. Step 4 If you haven't found any information, look at the pictures.
3 **The draft plan was revised through a series of student discussions**	Added: New Step 1: Think of a topic and find a book. New Step 5: If you haven't found any words, start skimming (a quick look at the words). New Step 6: If you still haven't found anything, look for another book on the topic. New Step 7: When you have found it, read it. New Step 8: Write it down in your own words.
4 **Students considered whether there was a need to re-order the steps**	Reversed: Steps 3 and 4. Changed: Steps 3 and 4. Step 3: Look in the contents for your topic. Step 4: Look in the index for your topic.
5 **Students then exchanged books with their neighbours to test the plan**	
6 **Review**	Students realized there were too many acting steps and no checking or thinking steps, and changed their plan steps. An end step was included to conclude the task.
7 **Students trialled the plan in the following lesson** The final plan read:	1 Think of a topic and find a book. 2 Read the title. 3 Where will I find the information? 4 If I haven't found any information, look at the pictures.

> 5 If I haven't found any pictures start
>   skimming (a quick look at the writing).
> 6 If no information, find a new book.
> 7 Write the information in my own words.
> 8 Check my setting out.
> 9 Keep information to include in project.

required. For example, a plan for two-column addition with carrying learned as a numeration task can be applied to oral and written word problems, or to calculations using money or linear measurement. At the classroom interaction level, this phase involves the movement from overt teacher control of plan building to increased student participation in the plan development (i.e., planning) process. One result of this increased student involvement is the more pervasive use of student language at the establishment phase than often occurs during the introduction phase.

The three teaching–learning strategies are employed in this phase as before. Orientation may play a minor role, especially as students become more accustomed to using plans in their lessons. Orientation may be achieved quite simply: 'Today, we're going to make a plan which will help us. . . . You remember that plans help us move step-by-step through a problem so that we can get the right answer at the end.'

The acquisition and application strategies take on major roles as they provide the 'instruction' for independent plan building, and experience for the students to use plans in appropriate circumstances. Changing from a strong teacher focus to a student focus in plan development is often characteristic of the establishment phase. An example of this is given in Box 6.5. This Grade 4 teacher had always made plans which were not adapted by students. The school PBI coordinator urged her to allow students to take more responsibility for plan development, and Box 6.5 outlines a lesson in which the previous (not very successful) teacher plan for researching was being replaced by a student plan for finding project information.

The process outlined in Box 6.5 is a good example of an acquisition strategy that demonstrates students' involvement in deciding the layout and sequence of the plan. The use of sentences in the plan retained the teacher's belief in making the steps as explicit as possible – this might change over time to a telegraphic format that would simply cue actions and thoughts. This classroom activity extended over a twenty-minute period. In the secondary school, a similar approach might have been used, but the process may have been more rapid. In addition, the adaptation of a teacher's plan might occur at the level of the individual student, rather than with a group.

The application strategy in this phase emphasizes the need to expose students to plan use in a wide variety of learning situations. Plans may be written in individual student plan books, on worksheets, or in students' workbooks. This phase ensures that the novelty of plans is maintained to a certain extent when related curriculum tasks are attempted.

REFINING PLANS FOR CLASSROOM USE

In Chapter 5, we mentioned that plans can be made to develop skills which lead to more methodical approaches to general activities such as research and study. As students become familiar with the planning process they will gain an awareness of the organizational function of plans. If initial plans centre on curriculum content, the establishment phase provides the opportunity for students and teachers to develop plans that have an organizational focus.

Students who have difficulty developing plans in curriculum areas, or who are resistant to curriculum content, frequently are prepared to develop plans that relate to classroom activities, projects and homework assignment or non-academic tasks (e.g., the plan for cleaning my dog in Box 4.6 on page 72). Box 6.5 shows the development of a plan for students' research which may be implemented in small groups. Plans such as these have the advantage of taking the focus away from the need for success on academic tasks, while maintaining the high visibility of plans used within the classroom.

More on the purpose of plans

Students are not always aware of the connection between the plan and the task for which the plan has been made. Some teachers spend considerable time developing plans with their students on the blackboard and then set an exercise – or pass out a worksheet – to be completed by the students independently. When they move around the class to monitor students' progress, the teacher finds that only a small number of students are actually using the plan displayed on the blackboard. The remaining students do not understand the purpose of the plan and believe that once the teacher has stopped teaching and they are required to work independently, the plan has no further use. We have seen this occur many times. The teacher must impress upon students the importance of the plan, and that using the plan is not cheating.

Here are a number of suggestions that teachers can consider when helping students to see the value of using plans for solving problems. First, be as explicit as possible about the connection between the plan and task success. Second, make sure that students copy the working plan into their books or on to the worksheet before they start an exercise for which a plan has been prepared. Third, deliberately encourage students to use the plan, and reinforce those who are clearly following the steps in the plan. Finally, at the end of each teaching unit, discuss the value of the plan with the students, pointing out that success is often dependent upon their use of a plan.

More on using, and not using, plans

Plan development, use and adaptation exemplify the planning process. Using and modelling plan use will ultimately instil, and strengthen, students' knowledge of planning.

The effect of plan use is demonstrated most clearly when:

- introducing a new skill or procedure to the students in a whole-class lesson – plan development helps students comprehend the process and procedure;
- consolidating a newly taught skill or procedure using worksheets or similar classroom activities – the plan becomes the guide for task completion; and
- teaching organizational processes such as library research, study skills, or completing homework or other assignments – the use of the plan for complex activities demonstrates adaptability.

However, it is valuable to remember that there are times when using a plan may not be appropriate, as in the examples below:

- at the early childhood level – learning one's address and phone number;
- at the early primary level – knowing the rule for finding the area of a square;
- at the late primary or early high school level – knowing spelling rules; and
- at the middle high school level – knowing the formulae for compounds in chemistry.

Furthermore, over-using plans will make PBI tedious for teachers and students, weakening the impact of a small number of carefully developed and well-presented plans on students' understanding of the planning process.

Trying to make a plan for every classroom activity is inconsistent with the teaching–learning principles which underlie PBI.

Here are some points to consider that will make plan development, use and adaptation more successful:

- Ensure that you have introduced the concepts of plans and planning to students before you begin to use PBI plans in lessons. If students do not understand the concept, they will not understand how to use plans correctly.
- Use plans so that they will have most impact – using plans for every classroom activity will discourage their use by students, and may lead to confusion.
- If you have trouble making a plan, check that the task or activity is one for which a PBI plan is needed.

- Always link the plan to a task or activity that will reinforce a skill or procedure that you have taught – this will reinforce the relevance of plans.
- Make sure that colleagues who also teach your students know that you are using PBI – this may help ensure that students are not being encouraged to use plans in one class and discouraged in another.
- Ensure that your plans are age- and content-appropriate.

More on the presentation of plans

Presentation is not just a matter of creating a visually appealing plan, but it is a good start. Clarity of ideas is enhanced if material is visually well-structured. On a number of occasions we have been asked to help re-structure plans which do not seem to be working. The words and ideas are often fine but the problem lies in the presentation. Plans must not only provide the *information* for students, but they should also be *easy to follow*. Consider the student plan in Box 6.6.

Box 6.6 Robyn's initial plan for writing a story

The student who made this plan copied it from a teacher-made prototype on the blackboard but changed it into her own words. It did not work! The teacher helped the girl to rewrite the plan. It became more visually appealing and the teacher and student negotiated a number of minor amendments, as shown in Box 6.7 below.

Some teacher plans may also benefit from redrafting. Plans that are excessively long are often confusing for students. Look at the plan in Box 6.8. This plan was made by an experienced Grade 4/5 teacher who had been using PBI for about eight months.

Box 6.7 Robyn's amended plan for writing a story

Writing a story.

Think   What do I want to write about?
         What title will I use?
         What do I need before I start?

Do   Get anything I need
         (book, pencil, ruler, pen, rubber)
         Write an outline / what headings
         Write the story

Check.   Reread as I write
         Punctuation, spelling, capitals
         Do I need to add anything?

Hand in For marking

While it contains the cuing, acting, monitoring and verifying components, the plan might have been improved by reducing the number of steps. The teacher might have amended the prototype before asking the students how it could be abbreviated. This may have led to a more metacognitive plan which required them to make decisions, rather than only performing actions. Of course, there may also be times when a teacher may wish to show students how to trim a plan, and one similar to the multiplication plan in Box 6.8 might be perfectly suited to this.

Longer plans may also benefit students who are slow learners who may need additional sub-steps to clarify the connection between one step and the next. Box 6.9 gives an example for writing a business letter.

These sub-steps are often actions which relate to the main points. Importantly, they clarify the purpose of the steps, enabling the student to move unaided from one step to the next.

A way of presenting plans so that they are appropriate for all students in a class is to colour code the steps. For example, the main steps may be coded in red while others are in blue. Category A and some B learners may need only the red steps, while other Category B and Category C learners may need to follow all of the steps (those in red and those in blue) to succeed. Colour coding allows all students to use the same plan, without any obvious discrimination in student ability levels.

Box 6.8 A teacher's plan for multiplication

GOAL : For chn to be able to competently
'x' using 2 digit numbers.

READ

$$24$$
$$\times 32$$

ACTING → Steps.

    1. X ones by ones → 2 ones × 4 ones
                         = 8 ones
  ＊2. Regroup Tens with Tens
    3. X ones by tens → 8 2 ones × 2 tens
    3·5 Add Carry figure = 4 tens

Monitor →
$$24$$
$$\times 32$$
$$\overline{48}$$
→ Is it working
     Yes → Go to 4.
     No → Go to 1.

    4. Automatically place 'O' in ones
       place

    5. X Tens × Ones → 3 tens × 4 ones
                    = 12 tens

    6. Regroup Tens in Tens column.

    7. X Tens by Tens → 3 tens × ? tens
                 = 6 Tens

    8. Add Regrouped Number.

    9. Place answer.

$$24$$
$$\times 32$$
$$\overline{48}$$

Monitor →
$$+720$$
Is it correct
Yes →⁸⁰ on

    10. Add both Answers
       together to have a Total

$$24$$
$$\times 32$$
$$\overline{48}$$
$$+720$$

Monitor → $$\overline{768}$$

Verify → Check with Calculator
    Correct ✓
    Incorrect × → Step 1

Box 6.9 A plan for writing a business letter

What will the letter look like?
What does a business letter look like?
Collect materials I need (pen, paper, eraser)

What information do I give about the sender?
Address in top right corner
Write date below address

Who will receive the letter?
Write business address on the left side
Put name, address, postcode
Write 'Dear Sir/madam' under the address

What information will I be giving?
What is the letter to be about?
Make paragraphs, if needed
Check spelling, punctuation
Read the letter to check that it makes sense

Finish the letter
Write 'Yours faithfully' and sign it
Print my name under signature
Reread the whole letter for mistakes

Share the letter with classmates

USING PBI FLEXIBLY

As PBI becomes established within the classroom through the systematic application of the planning process, it is timely to consider how students are to achieve maximum benefit – even those who may be experiencing learning problems. As students' planning skills are developed, teachers can experiment with a number of teaching and learning strategies that can be used in primary and secondary classrooms with similar effects.

Student tutoring

The student body is a valuable teaching resource in the classroom. Students may act as tutors to other students in the class or group, but care must be taken to ensure that the same students do not always act as tutors, or that the same students are always the tutees.[1]

Group work

Groups in which all students take turns at teaching (reciprocal teaching) provide the opportunity for all to learn the role of the teacher and to benefit

It is better to have the tutor and tutee one ability level apart rather than have the top students tutor the bottom students.

from discussions with peers. By using group work, the teacher ensures that the language of teaching and learning is most compatible with the students – it is in the students' own words. By changing the composition of groups for different tasks or activities – by varying the ability, social, and interest factors – all students will eventually have the opportunity to work with others. Within the context of PBI, this mixing process gives all students the chance to see how their classmates develop, use and adapt plans, thus reinforcing their use through peer modelling.

In an earlier chapter we discussed the integration into regular classes of students with special needs. These students may require more of your time to help them to learn how to use and apply plans. The group work techniques may be of value when there is a spirit of cooperation and support among students in the class, but care must be taken to ensure that the group experiences are positive for all concerned. In addition, the use of individual tutors from within the class or from other classes may assist in reinforcing skills introduced by the teacher.

Working with aides, other teachers and volunteers

A second pair of capable hands is always of great value in any classroom but not all teachers require – or necessarily appreciate – the support of a consultant or specialist. An aide who can assist in supervising groups of students who are involved in developing or applying plans, frees the class teacher to work with another group of students or an individual. If an aide is not available, parent or community helpers may be an alternative source of assistance. These volunteers will require some introduction to Process-Based Instruction, especially to the characteristics of PBI plans and the expectations of student performance.

When other teachers – such as resource or remedial teachers – are available, they may work with the weak students (or with the remainder of the class), again freeing the class teacher to target specific children or problems. A similar situation can occur in a class in which there is a wide range of student abilities, or in a composite grades class. Specialist learning difficulties teachers may provide intensive training in plan use for students experiencing difficulties, although this training is often more effective when done in conjunction with the class teacher, rather than independently in a withdrawal setting.

Consulting with colleagues

Any innovative approach is more successful when a teacher can work with others. Each teacher will have a different level of initial success and have different needs on an ongoing basis. Where individual teachers can discuss their problems with other staff members, the network which is formed will provide the support to keep all class programmes progressing. If the school has a number of teachers involved in PBI, one may take on the role of school PBI coordinator. This role can be an active one – keeping staff informed of the activities in specific classes, providing classroom support as needed (and requested) and keeping a collection of plans across grades – or a passive one, simply distributing information on PBI as it is received, or giving feedback to colleagues who are experiencing success or difficulty, when they request it. In some schools, teachers have encouraged their students to move between classes of the same or different grades, to share the plans that they have developed.

Being aware of how colleagues are using PBI will maintain the momentum of PBI and ensure that students and teachers are exposed to a wide range of planning experiences. Table 6.5 provides a checklist of skills that should be present at the completion of the establishment phase. If you have achieved these skills, it is important to expand the application of plans and planning beyond the limited range of curriculum tasks encountered in the initial phases.

Table 6.5 Checklist for establishment phase

1 Have you encouraged students to apply plans to similar curriculum tasks?
2 Have you used orientation, acquisition and application strategies in your teaching of plans?
3 Have you encouraged students to take responsibility for developing plans, rather than relying on teacher-made plans?
4 Have students independently applied plans outside the original context, rather than relying on teacher-prompting to do so?
5 Do you encourage the display of plans on worksheets, in student work books and around the room?
6 Are students aware of the need to have cuing, acting, monitoring and verifying components in their plans?
7 Are the students ready to apply plans more broadly within the current curriculum area and across curriculum areas?

If the answers to these questions are 'Yes', PBI will be well-established in your classroom. If this is not the case, or if you are concerned at the rate of student progress, it may be worthwhile to re-read this chapter while thinking about how you can apply the ideas to your teaching situation.

SUMMARY

In this chapter we have discussed the initial implementation of PBI in the classroom. We have seen that it is important to orient students to the concepts of plans and planning as they occur in everyday life prior to the initial introduction to a PBI plan. Practical examples will illustrate to students that a plan is a systematic sequence of thoughts and actions which have broad application.

PBI plans can be introduced using tasks which have already been considered in the class or on a new task using a teacher- or student/teacher-made plan. The extension of the initial plan through application to similar curriculum tasks prevents the welding of the plan to one set of examples and avoids the association of plans with one task or topic. The use of plans for developing organizational skills in addition to curriculum tasks will help students who are resistant to academic work, and may also provide additional motivation to continue plan use.

Chapter 7

Maintaining PBI in the classroom

In the last chapter, we discussed the introduction of PBI into classroom activities. This involved using the three teaching–learning strategies (orientation, acquisition, application) in both introduction and establishment phases. By following the ideas given in that chapter, you will begin to make students aware of the value of the planning process. By providing them with numerous opportunities to develop, use and adapt plans, they will come to recognize how this process can satisfy their personal learning needs.

You will recall that in the first two phases, PBI plans were developed for a specified task: for a group (or cluster) of tasks which require the same plan sequence; by the teacher only; jointly by the student(s) and teacher; and by students individually or in groups.

Chapter 7 will focus upon:

- how PBI can be made an integral part of classroom practice through the application of the teaching–learning strategies, the use of PBI plans, and by blending and abbreviating plans to make them more generalizable (consolidation); and
- how students can achieve independence in learning and problem-solving through their general understanding of the planning process (incorporation).

This chapter will provide information on the application of PBI at an advanced level, and you are strongly encouraged to ensure that students are competent in the establishment phase skills that are listed in Table 6.5. It should also be noted that not all students will be able to function at the levels discussed in this chapter, especially those who are young and those who are functioning at an early developmental level.

THE CONSOLIDATION PHASE

Consolidation refers to the use of PBI plans extensively within a curriculum area or across curriculum areas. This phase, therefore, extends students' experience with plan development, use and adaptation more broadly than at the level of specific tasks, or clusters of tasks which require the same plan sequence.

In Chapter 4 we indicated that the position of the phases within PBI (moving from the base point upwards) implies an expanding range of curriculum areas in which planning may be applied. The transition from one level to a higher one will depend upon the skills and knowledge already acquired. The ultimate goal of PBI is to develop students' knowledge of the planning process which will enable them to judge which type or form of plan is needed for a task or problem. There is no implication in the model to suggest, as students and teachers become more familiar with the planning process, that they use plans only at one level. The teacher or the students may still develop plans for specific tasks (ostensibly at the level of the introduction phase) while developing plans which apply to a number of curriculum areas (at the level of the consolidation phase).

Hence, the objective at this stage is the development of students' planning skills that will enable them to decide how to plan in the most effective way according to the circumstances. As in the other phases, orientation, acquisition and application strategies need to be kept in the forefront of the teacher's mind when reintroducing or refocusing attention on the planning process. You will recall the relationship of consolidation to other teaching–learning phases (see Figure 7.1).

In this phase we draw attention to the importance of reducing and blending plans to make them more functional and of wider relevance than simply to those tasks for which they were originally made. In this way, the dependence upon a multitude of specific plans is avoided.

Broadening the application of PBI plans

A fundamental change occurs in the focus of plans at this level. One feature of consolidation is the development of student awareness of the need for

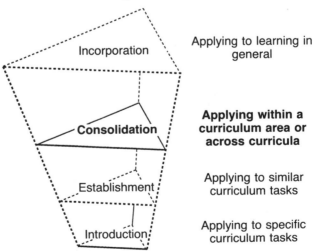

Figure 7.1 Relationship between the consolidation and other phases of the PBI model

decisions and actions, rather than actions alone. In this phase, plans must contain more thinking and monitoring steps than those used during introduction. Moreover, as students perceive the need to make those judgements, they recognize that some steps will cue a number of actions within the plan sequence, thereby reducing the number of steps needed. In other words, the student begins a movement toward monitoring or evaluative plans which check progress, rather than teach or guide. This feature will become more apparent as we discuss the three-plan applications at this phase: generalized plans, reduced plans and blended plans.

By the time students are prepared for the consolidation phase, many teachers will have applied plans in either mathematics or language arts. When plans have been developed in writing – such as a plan to write a sentence or one for writing a paragraph – they may be generalized to accommodate different genres so that a plan for writing will work not only for prose but also for poetry and plays. Plans for report-writing on specific topics such as Australian animals (Box 5.3) could be generalized to report-writing, regardless of the topic. Similarly, a plan for library research may contain the same steps, regardless of the subject area (see Box 7.1).

Box 7.1 A plan for writing a summary of ideas from library research

> 1 Locate the article.
> 2 Read the article.
> 3 Note main ideas/key words (on jotter).
> 4 Can I use these notes to rewrite the information?
> 5 Go away and write.
> 6 Read aloud.
> 7 Does it make sense to the reader and/or listener?

An example of the minor changes needed to generalize a plan is given in Box 7.2. As you will see, the original plan dealt with plant growth in different soil conditions. The teacher worked with her students to construct this PBI plan for a specific activity. When the students had completed the assignment – after about a month – she discussed the experiment with them (in the process emphasizing that the death of many of their plants in the school garden plot was associated with their disregard for the plan). She wrote the original plan on the blackboard once again. Her orientation strategy was to lead a classroom discussion on other factors that might affect plant growth. The students – who by this stage were familiar with the use of plans in a number of subject areas – immediately responded that the original plan could be changed very easily to apply to other experiments. They suggested studies to examine the effects of sun, fertilizer, water, or insect attack, plus a number of innovative ideas dealing with the altitude at which the plant was growing, and the amount of ultraviolet light and

Box 7.2 Two plans for comparing plant growth

Original planting plan: 'Comparing plant growth in different soils'
1 Think about what outcomes are expected.
2 Choose different soils (sand, soil, stones).
3 Plant – keep same sunlight and water for all.
4 Measure and chart growth every two days.
5 Are conditions unchanged?
6 Compare growth rate with expected outcomes (after three weeks).

Amended planting plan: 'Comparing plant growth under different conditions'
1 Think about what outcomes are expected.
2 Choose different planting conditions.
3 Plant seeds – keep conditions consistent.
4 Measure and chart growth every two days.
5 Are conditions unchanged?
6 Compare growth rate with expected outcomes (after three weeks).

irradiation it might receive. Only two steps needed amendment, Steps 2 and 3.

Organizational plans for writing essays in a specific secondary subject may be generalized to other subject areas. Such a plan would need to cue students to the objective of the writing exercise. Typical cuing steps in such a plan could be:

● What is the question asking?
● In what form does the essay need to be?

Although some secondary teachers may argue that the written requirements of their subject are unique, the similarities are greater that the differences. For students with a learning difficulty, a general strategy would be of great assistance. A homework plan specifically for mathematics (as in Box 5.6 on p. 84) may become a general monitoring plan by removing reference to the mathematics content and converting some of the cuing and acting steps into those which would emphasize monitoring (see Box 7.3).

Box 7.3 A generalized plan for homework

How to do your homework
1 What homework do I have?
2 What do I need to know?
3 Collect all the things needed
4 Do the tasks
5 Ask: 'Have I done it right?'
               'Is it my best?'
6 Get mum or dad to check

The plan retains the four key components, although Steps 1 and 2 are now both cuing and monitoring, while Step 3 is a cuing step. Step 4 remains an acting step, although it also cues a variety of actions, depending on the response to Step 2. Step 5 is a double cuing step and Step 6 remains the verifying step. The original plan was suitable for a student learning to develop and implement a plan. The plan in Box 7.3 demonstrates the application of these skills.

In mathematics, a plan for two-column subtraction with trading (as in Box 4.5 on p. 70) may be generalized to a plan for mathematical problems which is applicable to all tasks requiring the use of one of the four basic operations, whether the task is expressed as a numeration exercise, an oral or written problem, or a space or measurement exercise. The plan in Box 7.4 would be appropriate when introducing students to the addition operation, but it is much more likely that a teacher would use it when the students are in a position to make a decision about which arithmetic operation is to be employed. This plan could apply even more generally to secondary school mathematics if Step 3 read: 'What type of calculation is needed?' It is, however, more likely that the overwhelming majority of secondary students would not even need the prompting that a plan such as this provides.

Box 7.4 Example of the generalization of a plan for mathematics problems

1 Read.
2 Write the sum.
3 Look at the sign.
4 Calculate.
5 Check.

It is important to remember when translating task-specific plans into generalized plans that they must work; that is, the student must still be able to progress successfully through the series of thoughts and actions, to complete the task unassisted.

Reduced plans

Part of the movement from the introduction to the incorporation phases of PBI involves students' ability to reduce the number of steps in the plan, so that one step may trigger a set of action steps. In a plan for making pie graphs, the students in a Grade 6 class made an important change, which is shown in Box 7.5. Originally, they itemized a number of steps relating to the presentation of the pie graph, but quickly saw the need to reduce three steps to one which served the same purpose. The reduced plan reflects the

Box 7.5 Reducing plans

Original plan steps	Reduced plan steps
1 Read (the fraction).	1 Read.
2 How many wedges are needed?	2 Total wedges.
3 Draw the shape.	3 Draw shape.
4 How many wedges need to be coloured?	4 Colour wedges?
5 Colour the segments.	
6 Label the segments.	5 Presentation?
7 Label the diagram.	

ability of students to carry out the original steps automatically. Step 5, 'Presentation?', is a reminder to check that the original steps have been completed. Hence, the change reflects the strong monitoring emphasis in consolidation phase plans.

Blended plans

In the same way that plans can be reduced to reflect increased generality, they can be linked to other plans, to create composite plans for complex procedures. Plans developed for a series of information-gathering skills, such as finding information in a book (Box 6.5), library research, and writing may be blended to form a plan for presenting a research report. Many plans developed within the consolidation phase will be blended rather than task-specific plans, as students will seek to apply the planning process to a wider range of tasks across curriculum areas, and for developing organizational skills.

By the end of the consolidation phase, you should be able to answer the questions in the checklist provided in Table 7.1.

If you have not achieved one or more of the objectives listed, it may be useful to re-read the section and identify where you have been experiencing trouble.

Table 7.1 A checklist of skills developed during the consolidation phase

1 Are students developing generalized, blended and reduced plans?
2 Do plans reflect a greater emphasis on monitoring (acting steps being replaced by monitoring steps)?
3 Do students include cuing, acting, monitoring and verifying components in their plans?
4 Are plans being developed to meet student needs, rather than at the teacher's request?
5 Are plans being applied across curriculum areas and to organizational skills?
6 Are you providing for the needs of the range of students in your care?

THE INCORPORATION PHASE

The final phase of the model is not a teaching phase, so much as an application phase. Figure 7.2 suggests that students will have acquired the necessary skills to enable them to apply their planning competence to learning situations in general. Nevertheless, the teaching–learning strategies (orientation, acquisition and application) are still highly relevant, even at this level. Students need to be reminded about the importance of the planning process and of the need to monitor performance regularly. Parenthetically, it would appear that many of the strategy and metacognition training programmes reported in the literature require students to undertake sophisticated task and performance-monitoring activities (characteristic of those required in the incorporation phase) without the foundation that is provided in PBI. Some researchers have even suggested (e.g., Case, 1992) that children's cognitive 'hardware' must be in place before learning can occur. It is perhaps not surprising, then, that researchers have encountered difficulties, as students may be asked to apply a general monitoring plan without any clear understanding of the monitoring function.

In PBI, once students have a clear understanding of the planning process, they become adept at making judgements about what actions or decisions are needed to deal with the learning and problem-solving situations they

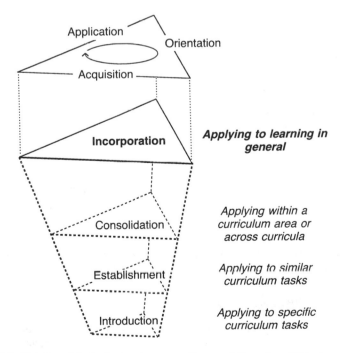

Figure 7.2 Relationship between incorporation and the other PBI phases

encounter in the course of their daily lives. They draw on their past planning experiences and on their knowledge of planning outcomes – both successes and failures – to guide their behaviour. The student who has mastered the incorporation phase skills will demonstrate three competencies:

1 knowledge of how to develop, use and adapt both specific and general plans according to the circumstances they are confronting;
2 an understanding of the influences that affect success in learning and problem-solving appropriate to their developmental level; and
3 an ability to anticipate where planning success or failure may occur.

As PBI is not a predetermined, rigidly defined (lock-step) process bound to certain achievements at the various grade levels, students are likely to gain experience using task-specific and task-general plans at all grade levels (depending upon the way in which their teachers mediate PBI). It is their understanding of the planning process that indicates achievement of the incorporation phase.

During the introduction and establishment phases of PBI, it is always useful for teachers to display current plans that students are using, and to store copies of old plans (in a card file, or folder) so that students who need to refresh their memories about some procedure may refer to them. When students are able to make their own decisions about the need for a plan, it may not be necessary to have plans visible (i.e., written upon a blackboard or tacked to a wall), as students will be approaching planning autonomy. As a consequence, there may be a tendency for teachers and students to forget to prompt students to develop plans.

It is still important to encourage students to plan and to use plans during the incorporation phase.

Teachers will need to identify situations that are appropriate for strategy monitoring, while encouraging students to develop specific plans when the need arises. One way to encourage students to think about the planning process at this level is to ask them to make a plan. The plan in Box 5.8 (p. 90) may be a useful prototype for this activity. An alternative would be to develop a general organizational plan that can be adapted to meet specific situations (see Box 7.6).

Continuity of PBI across grades

In most cases, students are unlikely to achieve mastery of the incorporation phase during the first year of PBI, unless they are older or developmentally advanced students. As a result, it is important to ensure that the skills of

Box 7.6 A general organizational framework plan

Daily plan

1 Think/talk about ideas for the day.
2 Decide on one objective/aim for the day.
3 Write down steps to achieve the plan.
4 Think about whether I've achieved the goal.
5 What changes would I make next time?

---

plan development and use cross grade boundaries. Having the whole school adopt PBI enables teachers to build upon students' planning skills as they progress through the grades, thus eliminating the need to revert to the exclusive application of task-specific plans for each new class (as would be the case if students were new to PBI). Whole school involvement also ensures that students who have reached the incorporation phase will maintain their skills.

Extending planning competence in the classroom

In this and the previous three chapters, we have discussed the process of planning within the context of the development, use, adaptation and application of PBI plans, and we have infrequently used the term 'planning'. The recognition of the need to construct a plan is an essential feature of the planning process. Introducing or reintroducing students to plans (the orientation strategy), teaching them how to make and use plans (the acquisition strategy), and providing the opportunity for them to trial, use and adapt plans (the application strategy) during each of the first three phases will give the students a constantly expanding understanding of how and where plans will work for them. At the incorporation phase, when the highly visible plan is no longer the focus, it is the students' understanding of the planning process that will cue their use of either a general monitoring plan or a plan for a specific task.

The incorporation phase really is a life-long phase, as it involves the application of planning skills as part of every person's repertoire of learning and problem-solving strategies. Rather than providing a list of skills, Table 7.2 provides a checklist of those that should be ongoing.

Teachers need to keep the concept of plans and planning active in PBI classrooms. Of course, as we have indicated earlier, nothing will depress students' – or teachers' – enthusiasm for any innovation more quickly than over-exposure. Maintaining the balance between sufficient and excess is a skill that teachers will develop as they observe their students' responses to PBI.

Table 7.2 Checklist of skills to be demonstrated in the incorporation phase

1 Are students applying a general monitoring plan to assess their effectiveness on a task?
2 Do students recognize the need to develop a specific plan when confronted with a task they are unable to complete unassisted?
3 Do student plans contain the four PBI plan characteristics with an emphasis on monitoring and broad action steps?
4 Does the teacher continue modelling the importance of plan development and usage?

If you have problems with the application of any of the above points, check to see that students have acquired the foundation provided by the first three PBI phases.

SUMMARY

In this chapter we have presented a number of ways in which teachers can maintain PBI in classrooms and other learning environments through the phases of consolidation and incorporation. At this stage, students move toward the ability to apply plans generally within the curriculum area in which they were first introduced to PBI, across other curricula, and on organizational tasks. Plans will become more metacognitive in nature as self-monitoring assumes greater prominence than in the earlier phases. A growing awareness of planning will be reflected in the students' progress toward self-guidance in their learning and problem-solving encounters.

Some students may take a very long time to achieve the incorporation phase skills, while others may never attain them. For this reason it is important to continue to use the PBI model across academic years and across grades so that it becomes part of both teaching and learning in the school and provides the framework which will allow students to develop their planning and decision-making skills.

Chapter 8

Plans in the social and affective domains

In Chapters 4 to 7 we concentrated on academic and organizational plans, as these are the main areas in which teachers initially develop and apply plans. We now expand this focus to include students' use of plans and planning within a third context – the social and affective domains. In doing so, we will concentrate on a group of students who are of concern to many teachers – those who, for various reasons, have difficulty coping with the educational setting and appear to be unwilling to cooperate. We will consider reasons for their behaviour, their impact upon the classroom, and ways in which the student, the teacher and the rest of the class may function with greater cooperation and accord.

This chapter deals with:

- the nature of behaviour-management programmes, including the emergence of self-management of behaviour;
- three criteria for management of student-behaviour programmes;
- the relationship between behaviour, academic and organizational plans;
- the use of PBI plans with younger students and adolescents; and
- how to maintain PBI plans in the social and affective domains.

The methods used by school personnel to manage student behaviour have changed in recent years, as the traditional notion of teacher control of classroom behaviour in the sense of classroom discipline has become modified to one based upon a belief that students must take responsibility for the management of their own behaviour. It is in the context of moving the management of behaviours from an external source (the teacher) to an internal source (the student) that the PBI concepts of plans and planning can play a prominent role.

'Behaviours' become 'problem behaviours' when someone – usually the teacher – labels the conduct and the student as a behaviour problem. There are many definitions of behaviour problems, behaviour disorders, and misbehaviour, yet few provide any indication of how a teacher might assist students to change their behaviour.[1]

Each teacher has a different tolerance level to disruption. What one teacher might accept as appropriate, another will find unacceptable. For example, some teachers may believe that students' chatter and movement around the classroom may be appropriate in art but inappropriate in mathematics. Some teachers encourage students to speak out in class, while others correlate behaviour problems with any disruptions to their teaching. For some students, the inability to understand the behavioural requirements of individual teachers, and to adapt to the changing demands of lessons, may lead to their being labelled a problem. The cause of inappropriate behaviour may lie not with the student but with the teacher when there are no clearly defined academic and behavioural expectations, when class rules have not been negotiated, established and accepted by the teacher and students, or when the rules are implemented inconsistently. If the teacher has ensured that the selection of content and teaching style are appropriate, it may be assumed that it is the students' behaviours that represent the behaviour problem.

Inappropriate classroom behaviour may be categorized according to the purpose of the behaviour. Dreikurs, Grunwald, and Pepper (1982), for example, provided a useful framework based upon four goals of misbehaviour. These are defined as follows:

Attention seeking   These students believe that they only belong to the class group while the teacher and/or students are prepared to pay attention to them. Attention-seekers dread being ignored.

Power struggle   These students only feel worthwhile if they are the boss, controlling everybody. Each believes: 'I can prove my importance by refusing to do anything you want'.

Revenge   These students believe that the only way of attaining a social position is to be disliked. They have been unsuccessful in gaining attention or demonstrating power and therefore try to hurt others, as they feel hurt themselves. In order to be recognized, they provoke hostility.

Inadequacy   These students see themselves as incompetent. They are deeply discouraged and no longer hope for any success or recognition in school. Their sole purpose is to avoid any further hurt, humiliation or frustration. They hide behind a lack-of-ability facade so that their real – or imagined – deficiency will not be obvious.

While there are some dangers in labelling student behaviour using any classification system, categories such as those shown immediately above have two major advantages:

- teachers can recognize students who seem to behave in accordance with one or more of these goals; and
- if teachers are able to appreciate social and affective behaviour from the student's point of view, there is a greater likelihood of dealing with it in

a non-threatening way by assisting them to disclose the goal themselves, rather than in a way that will take the decision to change out of the student's control.

Other approaches incorporate a belief that students must accept responsibility for their actions (e.g., Glasser, 1985). Glasser emphasized the difference between natural consequences and logical consequences. Although natural consequences are beyond the individual's control (e.g., if you place a ball on a slope, it will roll down), logical consequences are under individual control (e.g., if you call out in class, you will get into trouble). This approach requires students to recognize that their actions have consequences and leads them to decide whether they are prepared for these consequences.

More traditional behaviour-management approaches are based upon the antecedents, behaviour and consequences continuum. Reinforcement of behaviours is the critical feature in the maintenance or removal of unacceptable behaviour (see Alberto and Troutman, 1990). Behaviours can be viewed according to a number of sub-categories of off-task behaviour, such as acting out, physical aggression, verbal aggression and out-of-seat behaviour, all of which focus upon actions which disturb others. It is interesting that little attention has been given to withdrawn or reduced interactions that do not disturb classroom teaching but which are still educationally inappropriate. The traditional approach, therefore suggests that students do not comply with the class and/or teacher's expectations and, hence, need to be systematically managed through a discipline programme until they comply.

The responsibility for changing the reinforcement patterns which lead to inappropriate classroom behaviour rests with the teacher, who may employ behaviour management programmes that focus on token economies, behaviour cards or contracts to elicit compliance with class rules. Strategies can either be positive (rewards) or negative (loss of privileges, time out, physical punishment) or a combination of these (response-cost programmes). The key feature of traditional programmes is administration of rewards and punishers by external sources. As a result, the teacher may inadvertently replace the words 'you have earned X rewards' with 'you can have X rewards', which further reinforces the teacher's management of student behaviour, rather than students' adoption of responsibility for their own behaviour. Linking cognitive strategies with behavioural techniques, however, emphasizes the importance of the student's interpretation of events and maximises the options for behaviour change (see e.g., Galvin, 1989).

THE PBI MODEL AND BEHAVIOUR CHANGE

Plans which focus on social and emotional factors are applicable within all phases of the PBI model.

> Like those used in academic areas, plans for behaviour change are first applied in the introduction phase, even if students are functioning at another phase on academic or organizational plans.

It is unlikely, however, that students with behaviour problems will be operating at the consolidation or incorporation levels, as most will also have learning difficulties and are likely to be under-achievers (Conway, 1990). Using plans progressively through the four phases will require close teacher monitoring and systematic teaching and learning to attain consistent and positive student responses.

CRITERIA FOR PBI BEHAVIOUR PLANS

The PBI model is based on the belief that students must aim to attain autonomy in learning and problem-solving. Hence, PBI plans assist in the transfer of knowledge and skills from some external source (e.g., the classroom teacher, library resources) to the student. When considering the traditional behaviour-management domain, it has been typical that the teacher and students determine the class rules and the consequences of following or disregarding these rules. The choice of management programme to maintain acceptable behaviours has frequently been left to the teacher alone, who then advises the student of the programme and its method of operation. To be consistent with the principles which underlie PBI, we suggest that teachers consider the following statements, before attempting to introduce plans within behaviour-management programmes.

There are three fundamental propositions relating to the management of behaviour problems:

1 the students must want to change their behaviour if a behaviour-management programme is to work effectively;
2 the development of the process of change requires the active, ongoing involvement of the student; and
3 the process of change must occur within the teaching–learning context.

The first statement immediately above is based on the belief that we can manage behaviour only if the individual cedes control of behaviour to another. A student who abides by a behaviour-management programme that requires him to stop calling out in class or remain in seat has *permitted* the teacher to use reinforcers or punishers. In some cases, students may accept rewards for positive behaviour but refuse punishers for negative behaviour. Teachers appear to restructure their behaviour programmes to enhance compliance, although in reality they are restructuring it to ensure student cooperation.

Where students choose not to comply with the teacher's behaviour-management programme, the teacher typically sees only two options: change the programme to gain student compliance, or place the student on increasingly restrictive levels of involvement in the school, until they reach a point at which they are suspended or expelled for failure to comply. The

Box 8.1 Levels approach to whole school discipline*

Level[†]	Reason	What actions occur at this level?
0	– student is working cooperatively	– no action – behaviour shown as good or excellent on school report
1	– occasional poor class behaviour, such as not finishing tasks or being disruptive	– student interview with class teacher, year adviser to resolve problems – aim for student to solve own behaviour problems
2	– repeated disruptions in school – student fails to correct own behaviour	– parents are informed – student goes through school policies with year adviser – daily behaviour report completed – may be banned from school functions
3	– student continues to ignore school policies – no interest shown in own education	– student and parent interview with principal, year adviser, counsellor – not allowed to attend school functions – daily behaviour report completed – may be refused access to playground
4	– student ignores any attempt to help – refuses to try to solve problem behaviour – behaviour continues to deteriorate	– school advises district inspector and regional office – interview by school discipline committee – refused attendance at school functions – daily report seen by principal twice each day.
5	– behaviour is unacceptable	– principal discusses behaviour with parents, student and school discipline committee – principal may suspend student, subject to Education Department policy

* Common format based on school examples
[†] Some schools also have a series of levels above 0 to reward positive behaviours

first option can be reflected in comments such as, 'I've tried every management programme, but they don't work!' The second is reflected in school discipline policies – particularly in secondary schools – that place students on behaviour levels similar to those in Box 8.1, where the focus of management is on clear documentation of non-compliance as a basis of suspension.

Behaviour-management programmes that reflect a cognitive–behavioural approach recognize the need for a balance between preserving a level of discipline in the classroom and the need to obtain student commitment to abide by the class and school rules. While teachers often see value in adult-driven forms of student management, we advocate a more student-driven approach which focuses upon having the students accept responsibility for their own behaviour and its management, under teacher guidance.

Many behaviour-management programmes are developed with the sole purpose of regulating behaviour. As behaviour and behaviour problems cannot occur in a vacuum, so the plan for learning more appropriate behaviours cannot be planned or implemented in a vacuum. A PBI plan should clearly link behaviour change to context so that the student and teacher have clear expectations of behaviour during classroom (or playground) time.

PBI plans that concentrate on social and emotional issues will be more successful if teachers have already used plans in academic or organizational skills. Students will already recognize the value of systematic plan application, personal responsibility for planning and perceive a link between plans to help them perform successfully on academic tasks and plans for behaviour change.

PLANS FOR THE SOCIAL AND AFFECTIVE DOMAINS

In the same way as academic and organizational plans are sequences of thoughts and actions that lead to the successful completion of the task without teacher assistance, so PBI plans for behaviour change must also centre on thoughts and actions that will lead to successful functioning in the classroom, with minimal or no teacher assistance. As with other plans, cuing, acting, monitoring and verifying components must be incorporated in the plan. A significant difference between academic and behavioural plans will be that some of the monitoring steps in the initial behavioural plan may require external assistance. For example, the teacher might remind the student to keep track of out-of-seat occurrences.

PBI plans for behaviour change cover a wide range of management skills, not only misbehaviour. As we outlined in Chapter 5, plans can be developed for a range of self-management skills, including starting work, organizing space for group work or free time, and the completion of tasks on time.

Developing a plan with the student

The most effective plan is one that is developed collaboratively between the person responsible for the management of the student and the student following full discussion of the issues. If a student has a history of behaviour problems then the development of the plan may not always involve the class teacher. A specialist teacher in behaviour disorders, the school counsellor (school psychologist) or the grade adviser may be the key adult. In secondary schools, the grade adviser may monitor students with behaviour problems when difficulties occur across subject faculties. If class teachers are not directly involved in the development of a plan, they should be consulted prior to, and following the drafting of, the plan and should be kept informed of progress. When appropriate, they should be involved in the implementation of the programme.

Initial discussions must include a non-judgemental analysis of the reasons for the problem behaviour. Discussions may include:

- disclosing the goal;
- analysing the antecedents, behaviours and consequences;
- considering the student's behavioural skills; and
- evaluating possible strategies that could be included in the plan.

IMPLEMENTING A PROGRAMME FOR BEHAVIOUR CHANGE

When using PBI plans in the social and emotional domains, the teaching-learning strategies (orientation, acquisition, application) apply in much the same way as they do in academically-oriented plans. The first plan will be at the introduction phase level. Orientation will involve discussion of the problem, the consequences and the potential solutions with the students. An emphasis will be given to the use of plans as a way of assisting the student to achieve realistic personal goals. Acquisition involves the preparation and rehearsal of a plan for a specified self-management programme which will lead to the achievement of the student's goal. Finally, application will involve the consistent use of the initial plan in a number of circumstances, reinforcing the student's autonomy in managing their own behaviour and responses to situations which were previously disruptive. As the student achieves success with the initial plan, modification to it will occur. For example, the plan may become abbreviated, replacing actions and teacher monitoring with more self-monitoring steps than were in the original.

Using PBI plans to achieve social goals parallels students' use of plans for academic activities. Teachers should begin with the development and use of a plan for a specific behavioural goal (the introduction phase) and syste-matically progress through the levels of the model toward incorporation. In exactly the same way as students will achieve autonomy in planning for

Box 8.2 Development of a plan for managing behaviour

1 Support teacher (ST) and student sit together.
2 ST asks if she could talk about Mark's (M) concentration in class; he agrees.
3 Discussion on possibility of using a picture of headphone to remind him to listen in class.
4 M and ST talk about the possibility of developing a plan to assist him to be on-task in mathematics lessons.
5 M and ST discuss plans used in class and begin to develop a plan 'just for Mark'.
Note: ST had prepared small pieces of different-coloured cardboard for M on which each of the steps in the plan could be drawn. She used one colour for each of the four components of the PBI plan.[2] As they agreed on the content for each step, she would then hand M the appropriate coloured card. She had also prepared a collection of small pieces of cardboard on which she has drawn either headphones or an egg-timer.
6 ST shows M the small drawing of headphones and asks what word should be written to start the plan. M chooses 'listen' and he writes the word on the cardboard.
7 ST places the word and symbol on to the small board using reusable adhesive.
8 ST asks what needs to be done next. M suggests getting the equipment ready. ST and M discuss what will go on the cardboard. M draws eraser, pencil, ruler and a book on his cardboard and writes '4' next to the drawings, to check that the correct number of items are ready.
9 ST sticks the cardboard on to the board and places an egg-timer drawing next to M's drawing.

10 M and ST discuss what happens next, and agree that M will write on cardboard 'Am I ready?' as a check that he is ready to start.
11 M and ST agree that the next step should be a drawing of M working on a mathematics exercise. ST suggests that the egg-timer drawing should be shown to remind him to keep working.

12 M and ST agree to have a checking (monitoring) step and agree on 'How am I going?'

13 M and ST agree that the final step should be to check with the class teacher. M records 'Check with Mrs Thompson' on cardboard.

14 M decides to place a small box next to each step in the plan so he can tick each step as he completes it.

15 M agrees that in the next lesson he will check the plan and if the class teacher, ST and he are satisfied, the ST would have the plan laminated and placed beside his desk.

The final plan

The following day:

1 M and ST remove the steps of the plan from the board and read through each step as it is replaced on the board.

2 M (following suggestion from ST) agrees that his mother should see it.

3 M takes the plan to class to test it.

academic objectives, those who are working toward self-management will be able to use their planning experience to determine if a plan is needed for handling situations they find difficult, to determine what form the plan will take, and perhaps to decide what support they will need to ensure that the personal goals are met.

The first behaviour plan with younger students

The first plan will require a large amount of teacher assistance in its development, as students are often unfamiliar with the concept of accepting responsibility for their actions and for self-monitoring of behaviour. Monitoring and verifying steps may also require teacher assistance. When students have few acceptable behaviour skills, the teacher may provide many of the initial suggestions during plan development, but the teacher must also remain sensitive to the need for student agreement to the programme which is implemented through the plan.

Sometimes trial-and-error experiences may be the only way to refine plans which focus on behaviour change, especially when some students have entrenched behaviour patterns and have had little encouragement to work toward a more socially acceptable repertoire of behaviours. For other students, especially those who are young, encouraging their involvement in the self-management process early in their school life, will overcome many of the difficulties which would ultimately lead to major problems. In Box 8.2, for example, is a description of the development of a plan for a Grade 1 student with an attention deficit disorder.

The student, Mark, had been a source of frustration for the Grade 1 teacher in a large rural primary school because he was continually off-task. The teacher had tried every strategy she knew to maintain his attention, without success. Following consultations with the class teacher and in-class observations, the learning difficulties support teacher (remedial/resource teacher) brought the student into her own classroom to develop a plan for 'Commencing work at the same time as the rest of the class'. The boy's teacher observed the plan development activity and provided assistance and encouragement. It was agreed that the plan would be implemented in mathematics initially, as these lessons were slightly more structured than others, and required the students to work independently. Mark's class group was familiar with the concept of PBI plans and had already used them in mathematics and writing.

The first behaviour plan with older students

Older students typically have greater control over their behaviour than those in the early grades and frequently *choose* to behave in a certain way. For a PBI plan to work, these students must recognize that the concerning behaviours are occurring, that there is a need to change, and that they must make a commitment to work toward a new repertoire of behaviours.

Many programmes that focus on behaviour change at the adolescent level involve a tutor (school counsellor/psychologist or teacher) who works with the student to plan a programme that incorporates individual or small group tutorials and in-class monitoring by class teachers. Teachers may be asked to tick a behaviour card at the end of each period to show that the student has achieved the objective during the lesson. An initial PBI plan operating in conjunction with a programme such as this, should include self-monitoring steps to increase student responsibility and reduce teacher involvement. After a period of success with the programme, both teacher and student may sign the card at the end of lessons to rate independently or jointly the success of the programme. Ultimately, students should accept responsibility for their own behaviour without the need for external monitoring.

An example of a PBI plan for an adolescent is shown in Box 8.3. The plan is really a series of monitoring steps which focus on behaviour, and operates in the consolidation phase stage. It was designed to be part of a total programme in which the student learned management and coping strategies within a small group programme. Some readers may see it as a plan to force acceptance of the rules and discourage individual expressions of behaviour. It reinforces compliant behaviour thus reflecting the teacher's and student's realization that there is a need to conform to the accepted class rules. There is one further implication – that fighting the system will not achieve positive outcomes, only negative ones such as alienation of the teacher, and suspension. The second step is the common techniques of providing a warning of more serious consequences if behaviour does not change.

As discussed above, the plan emphasizes the importance of a two-phase response by the student – abiding by the teacher's rules (now) and seeking discussion and change at an appropriate time (later). An orientation strategy would be needed to teach the student:

Box 8.3 My plan

1	Behaving OK?	
	Yes – OK! No – read on!	
2	Consequences?	
	Change behaviour now – discuss later	
3	Behaving OK?	
	Yes – OK! No – read on!	
4	Think cool and calm. I can't win by forcing the issue.	
5	Behaviour OK?	
	Yes – OK! No – I've blown it.	

- the notion of consequences;
- how to assess your own behaviour accurately and honestly;
- how to change behaviours even when it's not what you want to do; and
- how to remain calm when you don't want to be calm.

Teachers may need to remember that adolescents who are having difficulties in the social and emotional domain often fail to see the sense of remaining calm and sitting quietly during lessons that are unmotivating, or lack the stimulating content of a video arcade. This situation is exacerbated when the classroom teacher baits or consistently criticizes the student.

MAINTAINING PBI BEHAVIOUR MANAGEMENT PLANS

Once a plan has been developed with a student, the teacher or behaviour tutor should aim to reduce the amount of external support that the student receives. The student should be encouraged to take responsibility for monitoring behaviours and to alter the plan to reflect a stronger self-monitoring focus. Plans can also be generalized to include all behaviours, rather than only the initial specific target behaviours. In this way students progress toward the establishment and consolidation phases.

SUMMARY

This chapter has considered the application of PBI plans in the social and emotional domain. It is essential that students take responsibility for their own learning and social behaviours. Contemporary behaviour-management programmes emphasize the importance of student self-monitoring and this is consistent with the basic principles of PBI. In effect, PBI plans provide a valuable adjunct to programmes or behaviour-management techniques which provide students with a framework in which to accept responsibility for their actions.

Chapter 9

Applications of PBI for school personnel

Process-Based Instruction has been applied to a wide range of teaching and learning situations. Over the past five years its application has been put to the test in a number of countries and in surprisingly diverse situations and contexts, although up to this point in the book we have emphasized the classroom-based application, as this is the educational context to which it is most commonly applied.

In this chapter we will discuss the wider application of PBI in schools, including:

- roles of resource/remedial teachers;
- use of a PBI coordinator in the school; and
- staff training for PBI.

In earlier chapters we described the conceptual foundations and practical matters associated with the introduction of PBI through the development, use and amendment of PBI plans. To a large extent we have focussed attention on classroom applications, as they provide teachers with a generalizable process which can help them work with students who have a wide range of skills and abilities. As we have indicated, PBI is not only an approach that will work successfully in regular classrooms, it will also adapt to a variety of individual and small group settings. In this chapter we will outline the manner in which various school personnel can use PBI and how support networks can be readily formed.

THE USE OF PBI BY INDIVIDUAL TEACHERS

In some schools in which PBI has not been adopted at the whole-staff level, there are a number of teachers who use the model as a framework for classroom teaching. Like many other teachers, they have established their own teaching style and classroom management practices, and have adapted the curriculum in their own way. These teachers find that PBI will work effectively, even though they do not have the benefit of daily contact with colleagues who are also using PBI.

One teacher in a moderately sized outer suburban primary school, for example, was introduced to PBI following a request for assistance with a number of children with learning difficulties. She was in-serviced over the period of a month by organizing two student-free periods per week when the remedial teacher took her class. In-class support was provided during this time to assist with the establishment of the teaching–learning strategies (orientation, acquisition, application) and especially to assist with the adaptation of plans for the students with learning difficulties. When the teacher was comfortable with the method and was able to use plans to accommodate the needs of all students in the class, in-class support was withdrawn, and only occasional contact has been maintained to follow her progress.

THE USE OF PBI BY RESOURCE/REMEDIAL TEACHERS

Resource and remedial teachers operate in a variety of contexts in primary and secondary schools, from individual instruction to whole-class lessons. They support both students who are experiencing learning difficulties, and their classroom teachers. In most cases, remedial teachers have a degree of autonomy which allows them to distribute their time in accordance with their preferred teaching style and the needs of the school.

One resource teacher has been using PBI in a large independent school for a number of years. The school staff was given an introduction to PBI as part of their professional development programme and the resource teacher recognized its potential for dealing with students with learning difficulties at all grades, especially those in the secondary department of the school. This teacher has been working in a number of contexts – individually with primary students, with classroom teachers to assist them in devising activities for students with learning difficulties, and team teaching a group of a dozen slow learners in a remedial mathematics programme.

When the resource teacher was new to PBI, she received assistance from one of the authors in developing a programme based upon PBI plans for her remedial mathematics group. As the majority of the teachers in the school were at least familiar with the PBI concepts, plan development and use in the classroom became a common occurrence. This teacher was then able to support others who began to incorporate PBI more and more into their own teaching repertoire. The resource teacher has regularly used the concepts of plans and planning to overcome specific learning problems being encountered by students. In this school, PBI has become an additional teaching strategy which is used by teachers as the need arises, although little attention has been given to the developmental progression which is inherent in the full application.

WHOLE-SCHOOL APPROACHES TO PBI

When all members of the teaching staff have adopted the principles and practices of PBI, there is a rich network of support and cooperation which provides encouragement and the sharing of ideas and resources. One of the major advantages comes from the consistent application of PBI across grades (the developmental progression to which we referred in the previous paragraph). It acts as a common framework for teaching and learning practices and it is the student population which reaps the benefits. When students progress from one grade to the next, the development, use and adaptation of plans is consistent, allowing them to regulate their own learning. In effect, their independence in learning and problem-solving is enriched and refined by the different instructional approaches adopted by one teacher or another, while the foundation remains stable.

We use the term 'whole-school approach' to apply to situations in which all teachers have received a comprehensive in-service programme on PBI and where a majority of the staff have opted to incorporate the methods into their teaching practice. While there are many schools in which all teaching staff use PBI, it is often the case that a small number of teachers will choose not to adopt PBI practices, for one reason or another. For some, the philosophy of PBI is inconsistent with their own; others may simply be unwilling to modify their teaching approach; while for some, notably those who are very new to the profession, establishing classroom practices and management skills is a primary concern.

Where PBI is in general use, we have found teachers to be very positive and the administrative staff to be especially supportive. In the early stages, when teachers are coming to terms with PBI, the ability to share experiences with colleagues is particularly valuable. One professional development practice which teachers have reported as being extremely successful is the use of demonstration lessons in which a plan is being developed and used. Needless to say, the demonstrating teacher may feel some apprehension having peers observing the lesson, but anxiety disappears when the typical classroom interactions between teacher and students become a reality. We have found that both the novice and the most experienced of teachers gain much from the discussions which follow these shared lessons.

> Without doubt, the whole-school approach to PBI is the most effective means of increasing students' performance and supporting teachers.

COORDINATORS AND CONSULTANTS

The continuation of any innovative teaching–learning approach depends upon its success in the eyes of the teacher, the students, and those who initially support it. There is often a honeymoon period with any new approach, which is characterized by enthusiasm on the part of teachers and, to a lesser extent, the students, depending upon their involvement. The initial enthusiasm may wane, however, if the expected outcomes do not occur; if the effort or time required to mount the programme is excessive over a period of time; or if little support is given to teachers and/or students to maintain progress or to overcome difficulties being experienced at the classroom level.

Being aware of these potential deterrents to progress, some programme developers have adopted a number of strategies: they have involved staff at the school level to develop a support network which would provide assistance to teachers experiencing some implementation or application difficulties; and they have divested the ownership of the approach to the school system, again at the level of the school.[1] In PBI we have attempted to follow this lead by developing support systems that are based within the school system, rather than with the developers. This involves three levels of support: the school PBI coordinator, coordinator groups, and PBI consultants.

The school PBI coordinator

Once teachers within a school have become involved in PBI following an in-service programme, we attempt to identify a school coordinator. This is typically a teacher (rather than a consultant or administrator) who agrees to act as a resource person for all teachers using PBI in the school. The task is not a demanding one – it involves remaining aware of how PBI is developing within the school, maintaining dialogue with teachers about their progress, providing assistance with plan development or lessons in which plans are used, and maintaining a collection of plans which have been found to be successful at various grade levels.

The coordination role is not necessarily high-profile. It is one which has been easily carried out by experienced or relatively novice teachers. In one school, a teacher with less than one year of classroom experience was able to work very successfully with his colleagues. In other schools, very experienced teachers have taken on the role.

Coordinator meetings

In a number of education regions, coordinator meetings are held up to four times each year. These sessions provide the opportunity for school coordinators to share ideas and resources relating to the introduction and development of PBI within their individual schools. Due to the support of school principals, these meetings typically occur during the school day.

There are a number of positive outcomes. These meetings are typically very supportive and the teachers involved are especially enthusiastic about the sense of cooperation, sharing and willingness of all those present to assist with any problems which are raised. Hence, coordinators receive moral support from others who are often dealing with similar problems, and each is able to recognize the important part they are playing in the progress of PBI within their respective schools. Of practical benefit is the opportunity to hear how PBI is being used across grade levels and to collect model plans which have been developed in other schools, which can then be shared with colleagues in their schools. These benefits also accrue to the coordinators' schools, as the ideas gathered at the meetings are passed on to other staff. An additional benefit comes by way of attendance of a regional staff member at meetings, who learns of the progress which is taking place within the region or school district.

PBI consultants and trainers

PBI consultants and trainers operate in a number of school systems. These individuals can be teachers, special education consultants, or guidance officers (school psychologists) who have gained an extensive knowledge of the theory and practical application of PBI through attendance at workshops and individual training. In all cases, they are people qualified to provide PBI in-service workshops or general information sessions or consultations with teachers, coordinators or administrative staff on the conceptual foundation or practical application of PBI across primary and secondary grades.

Consultants vary in terms of their direct involvement in PBI. For example, in one school district, PBI has been the primary teaching and consulting responsibility of the liaison teacher. This person is a support teacher who has provided a consultation service to all schools within the region in which PBI is operating. He has actively recruited schools and teachers, provided the initial training for teachers who are interested in the PBI programme, and in-class assistance for teachers who request help in applying PBI to their classrooms. In other areas, consultants provide support services to teachers and schools, either as their duty statement allows, or as an additional responsibility. Regardless of the situation in which the consultants/trainers operate, they are extremely important individuals. They often provide the initial information to schools about PBI, and are catalytic agents for its maintenance and development.

These three levels of support for classroom teachers ensures consistency in the application and adaptation of PBI methods across classes within individual schools (through the coordinators), across schools (through the coordinator meetings and the consultants/trainers) and across systems (through the interactions between the consultants/trainers and the authors). It is important to outline in more detail how staff development can be undertaken using this book and the skills of coordinators and consultant/trainers.

STAFF DEVELOPMENT WITHIN THE SCHOOL

There are six ways in which teachers who are interested in applying PBI to their teaching settings can gain the necessary information and skills:

PBI workshops   These are offered by certified trainers and are the most usual and the most appropriate ways of learning the what, how, and why of PBI. Sessions can deal with specific teaching needs and exemplify how PBI can help teachers overcome some of the more common problems being faced in schools these days. There is no other single, more effective means of working with teachers to establish with them how PBI may assist them in dealing with the needs of their class groups.

This book   We have set out to provide teachers and other educational personnel with a broad overview of the conceptual foundation of PBI and a systematic way to introduce PBI via the medium of PBI plans. Systematically working through the book is an excellent way to discover PBI. We hasten to add, however, that it is never possible to present all information, or to cover all possible circumstances, in a book like this. We highly recommended making contact with others who are knowledgeable about PBI, once you have begun incorporating the ideas into your personal teaching approach.

Working with a PBI coordinator/trainer   This is an effective way for teachers to learn about PBI, especially if they have not attended a workshop. There are many teachers using PBI who have been trained on an individual basis, their circumstances having been such that attendance at formal sessions was impossible. This is a common training procedure when a teacher without knowledge of PBI transfers into a school where PBI is operating as a whole-school strategy.

Demonstrations by PBI teachers   These can be of great benefit, whether or not the observers have been introduced to PBI. A lesson given by an experienced PBI teacher in which a plan is used will almost always exemplify good teaching practice. Discussions about the lesson will provide useful feedback to the demonstrator and valuable insights for the observers. However, demonstration lessons are not the best substitutes for systematic training through an in-service programme.

Working with PBI-trained colleagues   This would be a fifth way of learning about PBI. It would be suitable provided there was the opportunity to understand the conceptual framework – perhaps through studying this book.

Exposure to PBI   This may occur through discussion with colleagues, via conference presentations or published material (other than this book). It is the least preferred option as a sole learning strategy. While there are many sources of information about PBI, we have found that teachers and others require, at minimum, five hours of in-servicing to learn the basic concepts and to gain an understanding of plan development and application. Conference presentations and articles cover some of the more important ideas, but they are never intended as vehicles for training.

At this point we introduce the role of the PBI school coordinator and the PBI consultant and trainer.

The role of the PBI school coordinator

The school coordinator plays a major role in PBI by providing assistance to colleagues, as needed. The role will vary from school to school and person to person, depending upon the enthusiasm of the teachers and their experience with PBI or other similar cognitive education ideas and programmes. In some schools, coordinators are very active in seeking ways of making PBI part of the day-to-day operation of the school and its academic programme, while in others, the coordinators are simply resource people to whom teachers may come if they are having difficulty incorporating PBI into their classroom activities. As the PBI coordinator's role is most often carried out in addition to the teacher's many other responsibilities, we would not presume to outline 'duties'. Here, we describe five common roles; the first two are undertaken by most, if not all, school coordinators.

First, coordinators are typically teachers who are prepared to assist others when they are experiencing difficulties with PBI or plan development, use or adaptation. Making oneself available to discuss PBI with colleagues or to work cooperatively to refine a plan is not a demanding task and is one that can be undertaken during a recess or lunch break, or even in the class or staff room before or after school. Some coordinators set up a schedule for themselves to ensure that they make contact with each teacher using PBI every week or two. This will keep PBI bubbling away quite happily in the school.

The second role involves maintaining a clearing house of plans for specific topics, across grades. This is another non-taxing role for the coordinator and requires only the cooperation of colleagues to pass on examples of plans that they and their students have prepared. It is always helpful to teachers new to PBI to have an example of a plan first prepared by the teacher and the final plan which resulted from students' participation in the lesson. This exemplifies the dynamic nature of the planning process and will dispel ideas that there is only one plan for a topic or activity.

Third, coordinators are in an ideal position to maintain the consistency of plan development, use and adaptation across grades. By talking informally to staff, or through some formal discussion or dialogue, coordinators can determine teachers' comprehension of PBI and work in a cooperative and collaborative way to enhance their knowledge about PBI. In some schools, teachers have formed PBI interest groups, in which they:

- share plans they have used in their classrooms;
- discuss alternative ways of presenting the curriculum; and
- consider effective ways of dealing with students who have learning difficulties or special needs.

Fourth, coordinators can assume responsibility for in-servicing new teachers who join the staff of the school. Using this book, or the workshop manual which accompanies the in-service programme, coordinators can readily provide the background knowledge and some personal examples of how PBI plans can be used in lessons at various grade levels. The coordinator may also provide in-class assistance to teachers new to PBI, or have them attend a demonstration lesson in another class. Providing demonstrations and other activities will depend, however, upon the availability of free class time and support of PBI by the school administration.

Fifth, coordinators can play a valuable role in designing and coordinating projects which involve PBI. In some schools, for example, PBI has been included in the school management and development plan to ensure that there is a consistent and systematic approach to PBI across grades. Being part of the school development plan also means that human and physical resources can be assigned to the programme (such as release for coordinators to work with other teachers and to attend coordinator meetings). The school PBI coordinator can play a major role in structuring a school-wide approach to PBI by working with staff at each grade level to establish year goals for teachers' programmes and for student attainments. Providing a 'flow-through' of attainments will ensure that students build upon the academic and the planning performance as they progress from grade to grade.

In secondary schools, coordinators can become involved in adapting PBI to meet the demands of various subject areas. This may mean systematically working through the subject programme, or preparing lessons that use PBI plans in a collaborative fashion with colleagues. In this way, PBI can be incorporated across the school year and individual teacher will include suggestions as to how plans may be used in lessons. It is important that any model plans which are included in the teaching programme are not viewed necessarily as the 'right' way to present the content, but should be viewed as prototype plans only which will encourage teachers to adapt them to suit their individual teaching and learning styles.

The school coordinator plays an important part in integrating PBI into the school culture. Close liaison with PBI consultants and involvement in coordinator meetings will ensure that innovative teaching and learning strategies will transfer from one school to others, generally improving the quality of the education provided to all students.

The role of the consultant

The position that PBI consultants hold within their education systems will dictate how they can operate most effectively in supporting teachers and other school-based staff who are using PBI. A person who has been allocated full-time PBI responsibilities can, obviously, provide considerably more support than one who has other obligations as, for example, a student counsellor, librarian, or district or regional special education or language arts consultant. Nevertheless, each can disseminate PBI materials, provide information to staff who have an interest in using PBI, and assist teachers through team-teaching activities. All current consultants have played key roles in gaining system and/or regional or district support for PBI.

The consultant's personal use of PBI

All PBI consultants use plans in their day-to-day teaching or counselling duties. Those who have teaching commitments – for example, as remedial or resource teachers – use PBI plans in their one-to-one lessons with students with learning difficulties and in their support teacher roles in the classroom, where they work cooperatively with other teachers. Developing, using and amending plans in the widest variety of situations possible will give the consultant a broad understanding of plan use with students with diverse abilities. It will also lead to the accumulation of a large resource of plans which might be used if a teacher asks for an example of a plan for making a chocolate cake, a sequencing task with pre-school children, presenting an oral report to a class, or for undertaking a computer literacy exercise (to name just a few requests that consultants have received).

The consultant's role as resource person

Perhaps the most common role of the consultant is that of resource person. Consultants typically have an extensive collection of plans which they have gathered over a period of time from teachers at all grade levels and these may be useful guides when assisting others to integrate PBI into their classrooms.

Consultants can assist coordinators and classroom teachers by providing updates on new ideas and practices which have been generated and trialled in other schools, or other education systems. Staff meetings or grade meetings are suitable venues for keeping teachers informed about PBI.

In their training role, consultants will also be developing and refining new in-service techniques which may ensure that teachers understand both the theory and the practice of PBI. One consultant, for example, has refined the in-service programme to make it more compatible with adult learning strategies which emphasize mutuality, respectful collaboration and the mutual diagnosis of needs and measurement of progress. While this approach is likely to involve greater time in establishing workshop goals than the usual in-service methods, it will draw upon and recognize teachers' current knowledge and facilitate their assimilation of new conceptual and strategic knowledge. The advantage of this approach to the consultant is a greater understanding of teachers' backgrounds and personal teaching styles.

Team teaching

Team teaching is best considered as a temporary or occasional activity with any one classroom teacher. Obviously, the consultant needs to be in a position which allows for participation in the school programme at this level. A consultant who has teacher training may have greater 'classroom credibility' than one who was trained as a school psychologist, though the latter can work very effectively, provided a secure, collaborative relationship is established between the consultant and classroom teacher.

Team teaching provides the consultant with the opportunity to model PBI planning and teaching methods in the most relevant setting. This can be especially important when teachers are new to PBI, or if they are experiencing some uncertainty about how to adapt plans to a particular topic or subject area.

The consultant and the classroom teacher may begin working together by considering the teacher's instructional style and preferred learning activities and, then, by jointly preparing and presenting lessons which include plans. During lessons, the consultant can ensure that students participate actively and that they have the opportunity to amend the plans presented during lessons. This is an aspect of a PBI lesson which teachers may find awkward at first.

The role of the consultant in a team-teaching exercise is not as the prominent partner. Although they may begin by taking the initiative in demonstrating how the lesson may proceed independently, or at the teacher's invitation, consultants must always work toward the transfer of the primary instructional role to the classroom teacher and, perhaps later, to the students. The consultant's objective is always to assist the classroom teacher to become an autonomous and consistent PBI user.

The induction of staff

There are two roles in the area of induction for the PBI consultant. The first is associated with the recruitment of schools or teachers into the programme as a result of the dissemination of information about PBI. The consultant may then schedule and provide in-service training, based generally on the content of this book. The second role involves the introduction of PBI to teachers who may be transferred to a school in which PBI is already operating and where the school coordinator is not in a position to provide a comprehensive training programme.

The role of the counsellor or school psychologist

As counsellors have very limited time to work with specific students, they are not involved directly in the implementation of PBI plans within the classroom. However, the counsellor or psychologist has an important role to play in identifying planning difficulties, in establishing the need for plan use and in monitoring their use with specific students.

Specialist assessment of students with learning or social interaction difficulties may identify areas in which the student may be assisted (such as those shown in Figure 2.1, on p. 17). Students may experience difficulties in processing information, or have specific academic or behaviour problems which may result from teaching content that is inappropriate, or presented in a way that is not stimulating. Following this assessment, counsellors may suggest the use of PBI plans as part of a systematic remediation framework which can be carried out by the classroom teacher and/or resource teacher.

The counsellor needs to be personally conversant with the PBI teaching–learning model. This is essential if a teacher seeks assistance or resources from the counsellor if they are unfamiliar with its implementation or if a PBI coordinator is not available to provide instruction.

As discussed in Chapter 8, the counsellor may work with a student in structuring a PBI plan as part of an integrated counselling programme. Again, the class teacher would need to be involved in the programme and tutored in the operation of PBI plans, to ensure the continuity of the programme between counsellor visits.

The role of the administrator

The school principal is in a unique position to develop and encourage the application of specific teaching–learning strategies in a school. As the person with ultimate responsibility within the school for the management of its academic, administrative and financial operations, the principal can ensure the success or failure of any innovative programme, by the level of support given. We have found across numerous PBI in-service workshops, that principals who attend the in-service training and actively encourage staff following the in-service are most likely to have a functional PBI school. Principals who attend only for the introductory remarks, before retiring to their offices to deal with pressing administrative matters, are unlikely to have sufficient knowledge of the model to provide leadership in its implementation.

We do not recommend that principals take responsibility for the co-ordination of PBI in the school, both because of the heavy demands of their administrative and managerial duties and because implementation and coordination is often most effective when it comes from within the peer group. A more appropriate role for the principal is to ensure that PBI remains as one of the school's key teaching–learning areas, by referring to positive examples of staff and student application in staff meetings and parent bulletins.

Administrators at local, regional, and national levels also need to be supportive of innovative strategies and should seek feedback about the effectiveness of PBI from principals, counsellors, specialists, teachers and at curriculum meetings. Positive classroom practices will spread across schools when senior administrators recognize and support their introduction. Word of mouth often achieves this goal far more easily than submissions from people who are outside the school system.

APPLYING PBI IN THE HOME

Parents seem to participate more in school activities these days than ever before. In the US and Australia, for example, parents of children with learning problems are involved in the development of Individual Education Plans (IEPs). Parent volunteers also act as teachers' aides for special reading programmes or as student mentors. When a child has a learning difficulty, parents are often keen to ensure that the coaching which takes place in the home is consistent with the school programme.

PBI can be used effectively at home. Teachers can take the initiative to inform parents about how PBI operates in the school and may provide them with sufficient knowledge to ensure that home-based coaching is linked with the school programme through the development, use and adaptation of PBI plans.

Recently, a graduate student who was undertaking a project with one of the authors reported the results of a home-based PBI mathematics programme. It involved a ten-year-old boy who was reported as having difficulties in reading and mathematics (Gallagher, 1991). PBI was not used in the boy's school, although his class teacher had heard of the approach. The teacher and the mother discussed the introduction of a home programme based on a common mathematics test battery ('Yardsticks' – Australian Council for Education Research, 1979). The teacher reported that the boy thought that luck played a major part in mathematics success, and mistakes were simply evidence of misfortune, and often shrugged off. Both teacher and parent (also a registered teacher) thought that a major break-through could be achieved if the parent could help her son dispel the myth that luck played a part in mathematics, and could convince the boy that the systematic application of a plan was the key to success.

The mother introduced the concepts of plans and planning to her son using an instructional videotape which shows PBI being used in a number of classrooms. As part of the acquisition strategy, the mother worked through a number of model plans until the boy understood the concept. Activities were then chosen from 'Yardsticks', and the mother prepared an instructional programme incorporating plans for the various criterion-referenced exercises. Mother and son worked together using the plans to solve eight examples from each of the prescribed exercises. They then returned to the beginning of the exercises and reworded the plans into student language to make them more general (an example is shown in Box 9.1).

Box 9.1 A plan devised by a parent and her two children

Plan 504

To solve word problems involving addition and subtraction of whole numbers

1 Read the problem

2 Underline the words that tell me what to do

3 Write the sign at the side of the sum

4 Get a rough idea of my answer by rounding off and adding or subtracting

5 Do the sum

6 Check my answer by adding the smaller numbers. They should come to the same as the big one

✓ ? – go on

✗ ? – go back to Step 1

IF I'M STUCK ON SUBTRACTION turn to Plan 502 or 503

Working with the plans became a family activity, involving the mother, the boy and his 12-year-old brother. The boy was motivated to demonstrate the use of plans to his classmates, and he used a plan to teach long multiplication to his classmates. Reinforcement of the boy's work came from the class, who applauded his lesson, and from his promotion into a higher mathematics group. The mother's reactions to the programme are given in Box 9.2.

Box 9.2 Some comments on the effectiveness of a home-based PBI programme

'Brian has benefited from learning how to use and adapt Process-Based Instruction plans and is now convinced that having a workable plan beats guessing when it comes to problem solving. In the one-to-one learning situation, cooperative teaching was not an objective, but when the group was enlarged to include his brother, Dennis, (and sometimes his friend Chris) there was a lot of brain-storming over the best way to present plans, and there was instant feedback (sometimes a bit harsh if the others thought it impractical) and sharing sessions. The peer tutoring had a positive effect on Brian and Dennis' social relationship. . . .

Dennis proved a good tutor in the reciprocal teaching environment and Brian often found him easier to understand. Scaffolding was used for the earlier examples in each maths unit and was withdrawn as Brian became more confident. . . . Self-questioning was less easy to use although some was included in the plan, for example, "Have I remembered the carrying figure?" Did I automatically put the zero at the beginning of the second line?'

'Brian found the content and material of the program very relevant as he faced similar year 5 maths problems every day at school. Having a straight-forward and understandable (not necessarily simple) plan to solve problems that he was previously very unsure of, has lifted a weight off his shoulders. He was never at any time unwilling to sit down and try, as the benefits were very obvious to him. He knew that he was working in a way that he could understand and handle, to overcome a major deficiency which has been worrying and embarrassing him.'

(Gallagher, 1991, pp. 26–7)

SUMMARY

In this chapter we have discussed briefly the application of PBI both within the school and in the home. Having a school coordinator is an excellent way of ensuring that teachers who are using PBI can share their successes (and their failures) and help maintain a focus on PBI throughout the school. The positive support of the school principal is also an important factor for ensuring the ongoing success of PBI. Keeping parents involved through parent bulletins and parent–teacher meetings may encourage them to incorporate PBI plans in their home-tutoring programmes and, perhaps, also to increase their awareness of the relevance of planning around the home.

Chapter 10

Trouble-shooting in PBI

When beginning any new teaching programme, teachers may encounter a variety of difficulties. In this chapter we draw attention to the most commonly recognized problems teachers have reported and offer suggestions about how they can be overcome. We consider:

- why teachers have problems;
- a model for dealing with blockages;
- the need to encourage students' involvement in the teaching–learning process;
- the importance of maintaining progress;
- the assessment of planning and plan use;
- when plans should and should not be employed;
- when it is necessary to look at the teacher, student, and content variable to resolve the problems; and
- what to do when nothing seems to work.

A POSITIVE DISPOSITION TO CLASSROOM CHANGE

PBI is conceptually fairly simple. Few teachers disagree with the underlying values. They accept that students must know how to learn and how to deal with a wide range of academic and non-academic problems as they progress through school. Most also accept that there is a need to teach children systematically how to be better learners and problem-solvers, in order to develop the degree of independence that is appropriate for their age and ability. Learning about PBI and how to apply it within the classroom is a challenge, but no more difficult than presenting a typical non-PBI lesson.

Occasionally during training, a teacher may say: 'I already do this in my class.' Certainly, many teachers use classroom strategies that resemble some PBI techniques; for example, they may provide their students with a sequence of activities which specify how a task is to be done.

> There is more to PBI than simply using a plan for it is a means of systematically and explicitly teaching students how to learn and how to problem-solve.

As might be expected, teachers ask for most support when translating PBI into practical, classroom activities. In Chapters 4 to 8 we have provided some suggestions: the hardest part of the process is making the first step.

Having begun to use PBI, teachers may experience some uncertainty about how to keep students moving toward independence in learning and problem-solving. This is really the purpose of this chapter – to deal with the blockages that teachers may experience once they have tested the methods described in this book. If you have not already begun using PBI, this chapter might help you anticipate some of the problems that others have encountered – it will probably be of greater value if you have trialled PBI for yourself.

Let us first overview some of the objectives of the programme. PBI is intended to:

- help teachers confront and satisfy some of their needs when teaching mixed ability classes at primary and secondary school levels;
- sensitize teachers to the way in which students deal with the curriculum, from the students' perspective (see Chapters 1 and 2 for a discussion of these ideas);
- provide a systematic introduction to planning and decision making through the use of PBI plans (see Chapters 3 to 5 to refresh your recollections);
- lead to the progressive transfer of learning and problem-solving initiatives from the teacher to the student, under the teacher's direction (see Chapters 6 to 8 to review the process); and
- assist teachers and students to become more flexible in their approaches to the teaching–learning process in a number of educational settings (this material is also covered in Chapters 5 to 8).

In this chapter we have used a trouble-shooting approach – identifying a number of common problems and then suggesting how they may be overcome.

MAINTAINING PROGRESS

Introducing the concepts of plans and planning to students is the first step in the PBI process. Using plans in lessons is the second. You will recall that change is fundamental in PBI – change in the form and use of plans, and change in the sophistication of the planning process over time.

Some teachers begin to use PBI by developing and using plans infrequently, or for a very limited number of activities. After a period of time, they may not discern any change in students' academic performance or in the spirit of cooperation and involvement of the students in classroom activities. They may ask, 'I don't see what all the fuss is about. Is this all I have to do? I'm using plans and the children are using them too, but I don't see much happening that wasn't happening before I started PBI.' Other teachers have been concerned that they are not using PBI properly and say, 'I'm stuck. There's nothing happening. What am I doing wrong?' Perhaps the most positive aspect of such comments as these is the recognition that progress is stalled. If these are thoughts that you or other teachers have had, then this is the time to evaluate what has been happening and to consider how to regain the initiative.

REGAINING THE INITIATIVE

Regaining the initiative may involve no more than clarification of the purpose of PBI plans and their use. It may, however, require a more careful analysis of the problem and of the dynamics operating within your setting. Regardless, some effort will be required to regenerate lost momentum, but the outcome will be worth it.

When working through this chapter, it may be useful to have a pencil and paper on hand and to make some notes as you read. Sometimes the ideas we have when reading are lost through interruptions or when we encounter information overload.

We have developed a trouble-shooting outline to assist in the evaluation process. You will see in Figure 10.1 that there are two levels of assessment. The process can begin by recognizing that students are not responding to the PBI process. This may lead to two questions. The first, 'Is there a quick solution?' leads to a consideration of some obvious problems that can be easily overcome. The second, 'What can I do if the problem seems to be more complex?' requires a careful look at the existing circumstances of the teaching–learning environment. Let us look at the specific aspects of the model.

TROUBLE IN GETTING STARTED

Getting started can be the most significant hurdle for some teachers. Occasionally, some misunderstandings about the role of the PBI strategies and phases can lead to procrastination. If you are puzzled about any aspect, we suggest that you re-read Chapters 4 to 8 in which we describe the model and its application.

Some teachers are quick to begin PBI, while others take their time, allowing time for the PBI concepts and ideas to germinate. If you are still

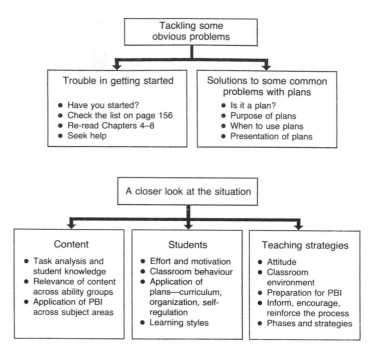

Figure 10.1 A model for overcoming blockages in the PBI process

in this position, here are eight steps to help you start using PBI in your classroom:

1 Think carefully about the curriculum area that will be most suitable for trialling PBI.
2 Ensure that you have prepared the students for PBI and the planning process by introducing the concepts of plans and planning to them – a classroom discussion is always effective (the orientation strategy of PBI).
3 Prepare a lesson and a work exercise in which students will use a PBI plan.
4 Present the lesson in which you develop and use the plan with the students – make sure they contribute to the final draft of the plan (the acquisition strategy).
5 Emphasize the importance of using the plan during the activity you have set.
6 Have students complete the activity – you will need to check that all students in the class understand the steps in the plan and can work through them unaided (the application strategy).
7 Use the orientation, acquisition and application strategies consistently each time you use plans in the classroom.

8 Set yourself a goal of using plans between five and ten times per term.

Setting yourself a goal and using plans consistently will help your students become effective developers, users, and adaptors of plans in the early stages.

SOLUTIONS TO SOME COMMON PROBLEMS WITH PLANS

Most often, teachers have reported having difficulties with making and using PBI plans. Here are some suggestions that will help you to overcome the more common problems.

Is it a PBI plan?

Plans are the building blocks of PBI, and success hinges on the quality of the plans. While we emphasize again that there are places for rules, directions and teaching sequences in all classrooms, it is important to be clear about the differences between plans and non-plans. Let's look at three types of plans which are common to classroom practice: teaching plans (perhaps more accurately called the lesson outline), teacher-made plans and student-made plans.

Teaching plans

Have you ever borrowed a fellow student's lecture notes and had difficulty understanding them? Most people do, because notes are made as reminders or as cues for recall of the information by linking new knowledge with information and structures that are already possessed. If you lack the existing structure, there is no way to cue recall or comprehension. Children face the same problem when they are asked to perform a task based upon a teaching plan or lesson outline. This is why PBI plans are so important.

Teaching plans are only meant to cue the teacher during the presentation of the lesson. Here, for example, is a segment of the outline that we used for writing part of Chapter 3:

Introduction to some important concepts:

- What is learning?
- What is cognition? (strategies, executive processes)
- What is metacognition?

Why we must know about thinking and learning:

- Building blocks of effective teaching and learning.
- The teaching/learning process.
- Identifies key factors in the PBI approach.

Cognitive approaches that you may know:

- Cognitive behaviour modification.

- Those that emphasize strategies.
- Those that emphasize metastrategies.

As you can see, this outline contains very little information and would not be very helpful to others if they were asked to write about the same topics. Nevertheless, teaching plans have a place – to help structure the presentation – but they are not effective instructional devices.

Always remember that the PBI plan must enable the student to move independently from one step to the next to complete the task successfully.

Teachers' plans

When preparing a plan for use with the class, it is important to remember that it should always be a prototype. It is essential that students give feedback about their understanding of the plan, and to change it if needed. It is also important to check that the plan contains each of the cuing, acting, monitoring and verifying components. Look at the teacher-made plans in Box 4.7 on p. 73. Notice that the directions on the left are not a PBI plan – can you see why? On the right is a PBI plan for the same task.

Both plans are directive (see the words that have been used: add, read, take away, calculate, check) and both are based on a number of assumptions:

- that the student understands the presented problem;
- that the student knows what must be done in each step;
- that the student is capable of performing the required arithmetic operation; and
- that the student is prepared to do the exercise.

The list of steps on the left is a set of directions and does not necessarily require the student to understand *what* is being done or *why*, and may in fact confuse some students. The PBI plan on the right assumes an understanding of the problem and requires decisions to be made: 'What type of sum is it?', 'Which operation do I use?'

The primary objective of PBI is to get the students to think about what is to be done so that they develop an understanding of the active role that they must play in the teaching and learning process.

Student plans

Some teachers get students involved in plan development right from the time they start PBI in their classrooms. This is a matter of personal style. Once students have the idea of the purpose of plans and how to go about making them, they generally become enthusiastic plan-makers. There are, however, a couple of points to keep in mind. In the same way that teachers may inadvertently produce a set of directions when developing a prototype plan, students also will do the same. In other words, their plans may not always be PBI plans.

Box 10.1 Putting an egg in a bottle

A student plan for science: how to put a boiled egg in a bottle

1. Remove the shell.
2. Screw some tissue paper into a ball.
3. Push it into the bottle and set fire to the paper.
4. Place the egg in the mouth of the bottle.
5. The egg gradually makes its way into the bottle.
6. Then the egg will drop in the bottle.

You can see that the plan in Box 10.1 is for a common science task which demonstrates atmospheric pressure. It is likely that the Grade 5 boy who wrote this plan could move through the steps, one by one, to achieve success. It is, however, a one-off guide and largely a set of directions. Steps 5 and 6 might refer to monitoring and verifying features, though they are written as descriptions of what should occur if the experiment is progressing according to nature. However, the steps do not explicitly prompt any decision-making.

Remember that students are likely to make non-PBI plans when they do not understand that a plan should prompt thoughts and actions.

Here are a number of ideas which will help you overcome problems in plan development:

- Check whether the plan you have prepared contains the four key components.
- Do not be concerned if steps are not clearly cuing, acting, monitoring or verifying steps – when plans are made for complex tasks (such as a plan for library research), each step may be multi-purpose.
- Check that the words used in the plan are known and commonly used by the students.
- Check that symbols or pictures used in the plan (and their meanings) are known to the students.

- Check that the thoughts, actions and decisions required in each step are known to the students.
- Check that the prerequisite knowledge for the activity is held by the students.
- Encourage students to suggest changes to the tentative plan, to ensure comprehension.

Using plans appropriately

Students are not always aware of the connection between the plan and the task for which it has been made. Here are a number of thoughts which might help students make the connection:

- Be explicit about the link between the plan and success in the task.
- Insist that students use the plan.
- Have students copy down the final plan into their workbooks or on to the worksheet before they start the exercise.
- Prompt plan use when students are not following the plan.
- Reinforce students who are clearly following the steps in the plan.
- At the end of each teaching unit, discuss the value of the plan for achieving success by asking students to tell in their own words how they applied it.

Occasionally, workshop participants have the misconception that plans are needed for all classroom activities. Use plans and model their application as this will ultimately instil, and strengthen knowledge of, the concept of planning.

The effect of a plan is demonstrated most effectively when:

- introducing a new skill or procedure to the students in a whole-class lesson;
- consolidating a newly taught skill or procedure using worksheets or similar classroom activities;
- teaching organizational processes such as library research, study skills, or completing homework or other assignments; and
- teaching self-management procedures which may be part of the teacher's classroom management strategy.

During PBI in-service programmes, participants develop and discuss their plans with others. Occasionally, a participant may experience difficulty when attempting to write a plan for a task for which a plan may not be appropriate.

Attempting to make a plan for every classroom activity is inconsistent with the teaching–learning principles which underlie PBI.

Over-using plans will also make PBI tedious for teachers and students, and weakens the impact of a small number of carefully developed and well-presented plans on students' understanding of the planning process. Here are some points to consider:

- Ensure that you have introduced the concepts of plans and planning to students before you begin to use PBI plans in lessons.
- Use plans when they will have most impact on teaching students about the planning process.
- If you have trouble making a plan, check that the task or activity is one for which the planning process is relevant.
- Always link the plan to a task or activity that will reinforce the skill or procedure you have taught.
- Make sure that colleagues who also teach your students know that you are using PBI.
- Ensure that your plans are age- and content-appropriate.

Presenting usable plans

Presentation is not just a matter of creating a good impression but it will always help to get the idea across to students. Here are some questions you might ask to focus attention on presentation:

- Is the plan laid out neatly?
- Are the words easily read?
- Have you avoided steps that are written as long sentences?
- Can the steps be grouped under headings that represent the cuing, acting, monitoring and verifying components?
- Would the use of colour or different letter forms help students follow the plan more easily or allow all students to use the plan at the same time?
- Are there some steps that could be simplified in a redraft?

A CLOSER LOOK AT THE SITUATION

The ideas we have discussed above should overcome many of the obstacles that teachers might encounter in getting PBI started in their classrooms. Systematically extending the use of PBI plans through the curriculum (or curricula) and into everyday activities will make the process of planning a common and effective mediator of students' learning and problem-solving.

There are times, however, when problems with the development, use and adaptation of plans are symptoms of more fundamental difficulties with the teaching–learning process. This leads us to reconsider the complex interactions between learner, curriculum, setting, and teacher variables – the total context in which PBI operates. In the next three sections we deal with a number of these interactions by focusing on the dominant aspects: the curriculum content, the student, and teaching strategies.

FOCUSING ON CURRICULUM CONTENT

These days, perhaps more than at any other time, teaching the curriculum means not only getting students to learn the content contained in the syllabus, but also the processes of learning. Hence, there are two considerations which are relevant to the curriculum: the knowledge the students possess about the topics being presented, and their processing competence. Putting the problem in this way implies that difficulties students may experience in the classroom are of their own making only. This is never the case.

In trying to overcome student difficulties we must consider the several interactions between the learner and the classroom context (that is, the curriculum, setting and teacher variables). The challenge comes in matching the learner with the context. As we saw in Box 2.2 on p. 22, a mismatch can easily be overlooked, and no matter how good a PBI plan might be, if the content is inappropriate for the student, the plan will not work. Where do we begin to look for a resolution?

Task analysis and student knowledge

The first step in the process must be to examine the topic being presented and its place within the hierarchy of skills (the task analysis). In classrooms where teachers have considerable flexibility in sequencing topics, there may be times when some of the prerequisite skills needed to perform a task or to learn a skill have not been consolidated by the students. Without this prerequisite knowledge, students will not be able to perform as the teacher would like.

Relevance of content across ability groups

One of the legacies of system-developed curricula is the assignment of a syllabus to a grade level – particularly in the secondary school – suggesting that all students attain the same goals at the same time. When the range of student skills and abilities within a class is broad, as in mixed ability and composite grade classes, the syllabus-grade bond is a nonsense because there are likely to be a number of students who cannot cope with instruction that is directed toward the mythical average student. Conversely, there are some students who already understand the concepts and who need extending.

The task analysis will provide the sequence of skills suitable for concept development, but students may accomplish the curriculum objectives at widely differing times. Teachers must be sensitive to student variation when using plans for specific lessons and may need to help students amend the accepted class plan (perhaps privately, on a one-to-one basis) so that they can move from one step to the next unaided.

If there are students of very low ability in the class, it may not even be realistic for them to work on an amended plan, because they do not possess the relevant prerequisite knowledge or skills. In this situation, the teacher may need to have the student work on a lower-level (or preparatory) skill in the task analysis. Developing alternative activities and plans for differing ability groups of students always requires some teacher effort, especially when other students are progressing quickly. In the same way as teachers develop alternative activities for different groups in the class, so plans may be different for each group. The alternative, however, is to have some students in the class who are not gainfully occupied and, hence, are gaining little from the lesson.

Teachers who have integrated students in their classes might consult curriculum documents for suitable topics or seek ideas from colleagues who work with younger children. In a school which has adopted PBI as one of its teaching strategies, teachers may have the added advantage of sharing suitable plans for low ability students. This may streamline the plan development process, but remember that the students must have the opportunity to amend prototype plans to ensure that they are fully understood.

Application of PBI across subject areas

There are two interrelated points which are raised by teachers from time to time: difficulty applying plans in more than one area; and concerns with the general development of students' planning competence.

PBI may appear to be more easily adapted to some subject areas than others. However, teachers have employed plans in most, if not all, curriculum areas: language arts, science, home economics, geography, mathematics, social sciences, history, drama, art, even sport and religious instruction. Teacher-librarians have also incorporated PBI plans into the library and research skills, and counsellors have used plans in consultation sessions with teachers and with students referred to them particularly for problems in the area of self-management.

It is important to move beyond the limited use of plans that apply to specific tasks only (in the introduction phase of the model) to exemplify the versatility of the process of plan development, use and adaptation. Primary teachers who begin using plans on curriculum tasks need to move toward more general, organizational plans and to focus on the application of plans to learning in general. Secondary teachers who begin by developing organizational plans need to demonstrate the value of these more general plans to specific curriculum topics and activities.

It is important for teachers to view PBI as a developmental process and, therefore, one which crosses curriculum boundaries.

> An efficient planner is one who can formulate an appropriate plan for a known or novel learning or problem-solving activity.

If students are having difficulty with the curriculum content, here are some questions which may help teachers ascertain the reason:

- What is the mix of abilities in your group of students, and is the level of the content being presented appropriate for all students? Being sensitive to the varying needs of students is the first step toward meeting them.
- Do students possess the prerequisite knowledge needed for success on the task at hand? Re-examining the task analysis may pin-point deficit areas.
- Are there a number of students who might have approximately the same ability and learning profile? The teacher might consider grouping children if they can provide mutual support.
- What are the students' strengths and weaknesses, curriculum likes and dislikes? Spending some time with each student as part of the regular routine of the day will help teachers to recognize areas in which the curriculum is incompatible with student competencies and to target areas where assistance is needed.
- Is there a need to amend plans and/or the curriculum for some students? In mixed ability classrooms, a specific task (or content) will not always be at an appropriate level for all students.

FOCUSING ON THE STUDENT

For students to participate in the planning process, they must understand the purpose of making and using plans and recognize the benefits of working systematically through the learning task or problem to achieve success. Getting students actively involved in classroom learning activities is one of the most important aims of PBI.

Effort and motivation

To build the desire to pursue a goal, the purpose must be clear and there must be some reward to be gained in the end. For some students, the purpose and rewards of school are clear, and it is an intellectually and socially stimulating environment. For others – especially those who have learning problems – the purpose is obscure and the consequences punishing. For most children, however, the goal of education can be translated into the frequently heard comment: 'You won't get a job if you don't learn!' Of course, the goal of education is far broader than 'getting a job'. Students – and teachers – often lose sight of the goals of education while pursuing the reality of the syllabus. For the teacher, then, stimulating motivation and maintaining student effort is one of the more significant challenges of teaching.

There are many factors which contribute to students' persistence and motivation. The relevance of the curriculum content and the suitability of the strategies used by the teacher are important, but it is the outcome, and the accumulated history of outcomes, which establishes the incentive to try.

> PBI aims to establish – and in some cases re-establish – a history of success. As students become familiar with the development, use and adaptation of plans, they gain control over the teaching–learning process.

This is especially important for students with a learning difficulty, many of whom have a long record of school failure and frustration. Establishing a pattern of success for these students, and indeed for all students, is an essential prerequisite for improved student motivation and effort.

PBI does not, by itself, make the curriculum relevant. It still relies upon the teacher to communicate the purpose and relevance of classroom activities. Over the long term, however, students are not only rewarded for their efforts but also come to recognize that success is a function of concerted effort *and* the use of versatile learning and problem-solving procedures.

Plans and planning for individual student needs

For the student to use a plan successfully, each step, and the plan as a whole, must be understood. One of the problems that students report is the inability to perform the action or the thinking needed to complete a step. Consider the plan in Box 7.1 on p. 119 for writing a summary of ideas from library research using an encyclopaedia.

If the student does not have the library skills necessary to choose, identify, and locate a suitable article from an encyclopaedia, or does not have the reading and writing skills necessary to pick out the main ideas or key words from the article, the plan is unsuitable for that student. If this is the case, the teacher needs to ask two very obvious questions. Is the task suitable for this student's abillity or current level of achievement? Does the student understand what is to be achieved by the task?

Both of these questions have more to do with the choice of the exercise than with the plan used. If the task is suitable and the student understands what is to be done, then there are other questions which directly address the use of the plan:

- Does the student realize that the plan is the recipe for completing the task successfully?
- If a specific skill is missing, can we develop this skill and then use the plan?
- Does the student have the necessary skills, while failing to understand how to follow the plan?
- Can we revise the plan, perhaps by increasing the number of steps so that the connection between the steps is more obvious?
- Should we teach a number of sub-skills as separate plans and then blend the plans together to form a general plan?

In most cases, answering these questions will put you on the right road to a solution.

Classroom behaviour

While PBI can help teachers overcome some of the obstacles that students might encounter when attempting to learn new material, it will not solve all of their problems. There will always be some students who will remain unmotivated and those who will have difficulty settling into the social environment of the classroom.

Teachers tend to be more concerned with minor classroom disturbances, which are commonplace, than overt aggression or defiance, which tend to occur rarely (Conway, Schofield, and Tierney, 1990; Wheldall, 1991a). Lack of cooperation, unpreparedness or refusal to work and student inattentiveness are three of the more common behaviours which annoy teachers.

There are a number of traditional classroom management programmes that may help teachers to deal with many universal student problem behaviours (for example, token economies, contracts, reinforcement of class rule implementation of a school discipline code). Alternatively, teachers may develop PBI plans for behavioural self-control (some examples were given in Chapter 8). These will tend to be organizational plans, for example, for getting started, or for staying on-task. The most important point to remember when using plans for classroom management is that students *must* be involved in setting the goals and defining the steps in the plan. A teacher-made plan for behavioural management is unlikely to be successful, due to the lack of student ownership or responsibility.

It is important that the student owns the behaviour management plan that has been negotiated with the teacher, takes responsibility for wanting to modify the behaviour, and sees that the teacher wants to assist in the process.

Plans for curricula, organization, and self-regulation

The student is the primary recipient of Process-Based Instruction, and the teacher's main goals are to develop a recognition of the role of planning in curriculum and day-to-day living, and to encourage the students to develop, use and amend plans appropriately and as needed. Changes in the quality of classroom climate are typically predicated upon the student's participation in planning as a normal part of the teaching and learning process within the classroom. When teachers perceive that there is little development in PBI in the classroom, it is wise to examine the student's response to the introduction and use of plans.

Adolescents readily understand the value of planning in academic activities. The difficult part may be convincing students that they need to formulate a plan before impetuously beginning the task.

Time taken in planning saves time and frustration in the long term.

Discussion and guidance is needed to overcome this problem. Younger children generally need a more lengthy introduction than their older peers. Demonstrating the use and impact of plans (and the planning process) in a number of subject areas and learning and problem-solving contexts will help. Through systematic exposure to, and experience with plans, children recognize the efficacy of the planning process.

The translation of teacher- or class-made plans into plans for individual students is one of the dominant ideas which sets PBI apart from many other teaching and learning approaches. One of the most effective ways of achieving this transition is by having peers help each other to make plans personally relevant. If a student is experiencing difficulty understanding the steps of a plan, another student is likely to rephrase the plan more effectively than the teacher. Students are also more likely to seek assistance from another student than from the teacher – though some teachers make themselves indispensable by being unwilling to allow students to make decisions or plan for themselves.

FOCUSING ON TEACHING STRATEGIES

From the the teacher's viewpoint there are a number of other factors to consider. Perhaps of greatest significance is the student's preferred learning style. Most of us respond more quickly to new information if we are given clear, concrete examples, but there are a number of style dimensions that teachers might consider (these relate specifically to the aptitude aspect of the 'aptitude by treatment interaction' concept that was discussed in Chapter 3). For example, does the student:

- prefer to work alone or with a group of others?
- work quickly to collect the ideas or need a gestation period to allow the new ideas to become integrated with the old?
- look for all the details relating to the learning experience, or merely those that are most prominent ('Give me the facts, just the facts!')?
- deal with specific details or want the whole picture first to see where the detail fits?
- deal with information presented visually more effectively than if it is only presented aurally?
- need encouragement to begin work or self-initiate readily?
- keep track of learning that has occurred (e.g., through the use of study notes or other personal memory aids) or believe that memories will not fail ('I won't forget that!')?

Attitude

Teaching is like most other professions – to be successful, a person needs to be committed, knowledgeable, experienced and flexible. To be a capable PBI teacher, the same requirements apply.

> The teacher needs to have a commitment to the approach, be conversant with the theory, procedures and practices, be motivated to develop experience in using PBI methods and be flexible in applying and adapting PBI.

As we have discussed earlier in this chapter, when there are problems in the classroom, they can rarely be attributable to one factor alone. Whenever something happens in the classroom – such as an announcement over the school public address system – how the situation is managed comes back to the interaction between student, content, setting and teacher factors.

We now turn our attention to the teacher as the primary element in the interaction. There are a number of points which teachers might consider if they perceive that PBI is not working in their classrooms.

Self-evaluation is always difficult, for it involves assessing performances from the position of an objective observer. It is important, however, because self-criticism (both positive and negative) can help us initiate changes when our best intentions and skills seem to let us down. Public confessions can be very entertaining, but it is usually best to review the personal world of attitudes, values, and opinions, and the effect they have on our behaviour, in the privacy of our own minds.

There are many questions that might address the issues of commitment and responsiveness to teaching and professional development. Two questions, however, will reflect the sum of all views, attitudes and experiences: What are the characteristics of a good teacher?[1] If you had the opportunity to choose your career again, would you be a teacher? These are important questions, because they allow for the comparison of our view of the ideal teacher and our personal attributes and perceptions. We urge you to take a few minutes to reflect on these questions before you read further.

Attitudes to teaching have a substantial impact on the way in which classrooms are designed and operated. Teachers who have attitudes and beliefs that sanction change and improvement are often those who are more enthusiastic about new innovations and incentives in teaching and learning. We are neither suggesting for one moment that there is an ideal set of teacher attributes or characteristics, nor that teachers should try every new approach which is brought to their attention. When considering any new approach, teachers must consider whether it is compatible with their own attitudes, beliefs and values, or whether there are some useful points which may require some reconsideration of the teaching and learning process in their teaching. These were classified in Chapter 1.

When developing PBI, we were keen to minimize additional preparation demands on teachers, and to present a model that encourages student involvement in classroom organization and decision-making. This cannot be achieved if students are alienated from the teaching–learning process, or denied the opportunity to contribute to it. It is not within the spirit of PBI to restrict students' input into the process, provided it is constructive and aimed at improving their understanding of the plans, planning and content.

From time to time, most of us take the easy way out in learning and solving problems. We are content to wait until we are told explicitly what must be done, rather than think through the problem for ourselves. Teachers can support this passive learning style by telling students how to do a task, rather than encouraging them to work toward the resolution themselves. We make the error of providing students with sets of directions, rather than requiring them to make decisions and set priorities for themselves. Thinking through problems reinforces the awareness of how, and how effectively, they think. Using PBI plans – for appropriate tasks – in place of sets of directions will strengthen students' independence in learning and problem-solving.

Classroom environment

How the classroom is arranged, where it is situated, and how the student and teacher interact can have a significant impact upon the teaching and learning process, regardless of whether it is operating upon PBI principles or not. In Chapter 2, for example, we noted that some students may work more effectively in groups than individually, while others prefer to work alone. It was also suggested that there are times when the teacher may choose a particular seating arrangement which predisposes students to work in a particular way (for example, in small groups or rotating through activity centres). Assigning students to work groups may be helpful if the teacher wants to give them the opportunity to develop PBI plans collaboratively or to reword existing plans in student language.

There are, however, other considerations which can maximize the success of PBI (or any other teaching approach) which do not relate to how the classroom is arranged but to its general physical layout or position. Here are situations which occur in some schools.

- Some teachers are disadvantaged by the small size of their classrooms, barely accommodating the number of students they are assigned. This has implications for the storage of resources and teaching materials.
- Some classrooms are encircled by windows, making them very bright and airy, but limiting severely the wall space which some teachers need for displays of children's work (art or PBI plans or project displays) and/or teaching resources. For PBI teachers, this could be a problem as we have emphasized the need for the display of plans from time to time, in addition to other exhibitions.
- In any city there will be schools that are located near busy roads which are constantly used by heavy vehicles. Others may be located near major airports or under flight-paths. The staff and students of schools in these circumstances have adapted to the noise, in many cases without any physical changes to the school. Acoustic insulation, double-glazing of windows or the construction of noise barriers seem to be some part-solutions which require funding.
- Some teachers find themselves in rooms which are adjacent to music or drama laboratories or to those of colleagues who seem unconcerned with the noise level within their class and oblivious to the disruption it may cause to others. In some cases, reallocation of rooms for specific purposes may isolate necessary (or unnecessary) sound sources, or a personal approach to another teacher may be another method of dealing with the problem.

In these circumstances, some creativity is needed to deal with classroom limitations. It is important to stress that adverse conditions affect all teachers and students, not just those using PBI. There are, however, some implications for PBI teachers intent upon maximizing the success of lessons in which plans are used.

As most teachers will know, certain times of the day are more conducive to intensive academic work than others. Presenting a mathematics lesson during the last period of the school week is unlikely to be considered as good scheduling in primary school, and history or geography lessons are unlikely to be as successful as they might otherwise be, if programmed immediately following a physical education class. Teachers might consider the time of the day and the expected level of disruption when they are preparing PBI lessons. You will recall that we emphasized the need for plans to be successful, if their value is to be clear to the students.

Here are some questions which may help you evaluate the classroom environment to maximize student learning:

- Is the classroom arranged in the most effective way?
- Is the arrangement suitable for effective student interactions, or for interactions between the teacher and students?
- Are there some physical changes which could enhance the learning environment and if so, how can these changes be made?
- Are there specific times of the school day which are more conducive to plan development and use?

When to introduce a plan

There is one last point which is worthy of mention here. Over several years, PBI has been introduced into many schools. One question we have been asked on a number of occasions is 'When is the best time to introduce PBI into a classroom or a school?' There are numerous factors to consider: the time of year at which teachers learn about PBI; familiarity with the range of students' skills and abilities within the class; the extent of support which might be available to teachers; and events which may interrupt the usual routine of the class, such as sports carnivals and other special events, to name just a few.

The decision about when to begin will always rest with the teacher. Consider, however, the optimum time but try to introduce the concepts of plans and planning as soon after training as possible.

Preparation for PBI

If you are using this book as a guide to help you introduce PBI systematically into the classroom, then we suggest the following:

- Complete Chapters 1 to 4 more as leisure reading than as studying.
- Work slowly and carefully through Chapters 5 and 6, taking notes if this is a help to you, and completing the mini-exercises for plan development in Chapter 5.
- Take time to prepare your first PBI lesson, following the guidelines presented in Chapter 6.
- Critique your lesson and revise Chapters 5 and 6 if needed.
- Chapter 7 will give you a good idea of the end goal of PBI and will reinforce a number of important PBI concepts.

- Finish the book at your leisure after you have started using PBI systematically.

Like most other teaching and learning programmes, it is essential to devote some time to preparation, especially when you are unfamiliar with the methods and their application in diverse educational settings. If you intend to use a plan for a specific topic, spend some time developing a plan which should work for all the students in the class. Make sure it contains the cuing, acting, monitoring and verifying components, write it from a students point of view, and then treat the plan as experimental. Think carefully about the way in which you will introduce the plan to the students and which of the students may have trouble understanding the steps. Approaching each plan in this way will quickly make teachers and students more confident about using PBI.

Blockages can occur when a teacher either uses exclusively teacher-made plans, student-made plans or shared teacher/student-made plans. A number of teachers who have discussed problems they have had implementing PBI indicated that they used PBI plans in much the same way each time. The outcome has been a significant degree of student resistance.

Students will get bored if the only way plans are introduced is through a teacher-made plan or if they are always asked to generate their own plans before they begin an exercise.

The maxim is variation – experiment with the many ways students can use plans, but try to keep the form appropriate to the task that you are asking the students to perform. Most teachers use a number of approaches when presented information, as they have found that variation in activities and in the challenge increases students' motivation, understanding and productivity. Similarly, changing the way in which students are exposed to the planning process will maintain interest and demonstrate the broad application of plans and planning. In other words, for some activities it is more appropriate for the teacher to present a plan for students to consider. There will be times when a teacher may want the students to think through a problem themselves, to generate a plan and test it. At other times the teacher and students may work through a task, developing the plan as they go.

The saying, 'familiarity breeds contempt', applies to the use of plans in the classroom. If you are concerned that you are not using PBI in a sufficiently wide variety of situations, it may be useful to review the several modes for plan use described in Chapter 5.

Inform, encourage, and reinforce the process

There are few students who will use PBI plans spontaneously after having been exposed to them during a class lesson, or having used them for a variety of academic exercises. Teachers must keep students aware of the planning process until they are familiar with it and its application in a variety of academic and non-academic areas. Reminding students of the purpose of plans is especially important during the early stages of PBI.

It is also important for teachers to model the development and use of PBI plans and exemplify productive planning behaviour – this is equally important for students progressing satisfactorily and those who are experiencing learning problems (see Means and Knapp, 1991). Talking students through a planning activity and seeking their input will demonstrate to young children the value of plans and the planning process, and encourage their participation.

Good behaviour management also emphasizes the importance of reinforcing the desired behaviour. While we see little value in developing a reinforcement menu and distributing Smarties or M & Ms to students who become good planners, there is much to be gained through praise and other social reinforcers. Once students are shown that there are obvious gains to be made from plan use (e.g., success in completing their classroom exercises), the likelihood will increase of their owning the planning process and using plans spontaneously when confronted by new or novel tasks.

Phases and strategies

As you will recall, the goal of PBI is to develop students' independence in learning and problem-solving. To achieve this independence, students must learn how to use plans in a variety of situations, both academic and non-academic. The mechanism for achieving this objective is plan use across the various phases of the model shown in Figure 4.1, on p. 57.

Many teachers begin PBI by focusing on the application of plans to specific curriculum tasks or topics, while others may introduce organizational plans first. Either option is quite a suitable way to start. To develop students' understanding of planning, however, it is not sufficient to limit plan use to specific subject areas or to the more general, monitoring processes which plans can fulfil. Teachers must encourage the use of plans across the various dimensions shown in Figure 4.1.

The teaching–learning strategies are the keys to the four phases. The model suggests that the teacher orients students to plan use (orientation) whenever a new PBI plan is used within any phase (this reminds students of the purpose of the plan), demonstrates the use of the plan (acquisition), and then provides a consolidation exercise through application using an appropriate activity. Application strategy may also allow the teacher to evaluate students' understanding of the planning process.

Getting an idea of how individual students are responding to the introduction of plans can be difficult when there are many competing demands upon the teacher during class time.

One way of gauging students' responses to the planning process is to incorporate plan development and plan use into classroom assessment procedures.

There are many ways in which you may be able to do this. The most expedient way will depend upon the grade level of your students, their ability levels, the content area in which you are teaching, and your personal teaching approach. Here are just two ideas you may be able to use or adapt.

Worksheets might include a section where students are asked to write out a plan for the exercise. This will not only give you an idea of the students' understanding of the process you have taught, but also it will show how skilful they are in writing up plans (see the example in Box 10.2).

A specific-purpose assignment might be set in which students make up a plan for a procedure you have just taught in class.

You can ask the students to prepare a plan for a task at the next level of the skill task analysis, which you have not yet taught. This exercise may need to be structured fairly carefully, to avoid a situation in which students practise incorrect procedures and it might be more suited to secondary school than to those in the earlier grades.

Here are some points which might help when considering the development of PBI in your teaching setting:

- When introducing PBI into the classroom, consider the need for adequate preparation of plans and for variation in their application.
- Ensure that students are reminded of the value of plans from time to time, especially when they are being used in a lesson.
- Use teacher and student models of the development, use and adaptation of plans, to highlight good planning practices.
- Encourage and reinforce students to develop, use and amend plans as often as possible.
- Ensure that plans are used in a variety of contexts consistent with the PBI model.
- Ensure that the orientation, acquisition and application strategies are used whenever plans are being used.
- Evaluate plan development and use by including relevant items in your regular assessment procedures.

Box 10.2 Worksheet incorporating an evaluation of a student's planning skills

Revision Worksheet

Calculating Areas

Write down a plan for calculating area

Use your plan to calculate these four areas

4 km

1. 1 km

2. 4 cm
    4 cm

2 mm

3. 2 mm

4. 5 m

SUMMARY

This chapter has drawn attention to a number of problems that teachers and students may encounter when implementing the PBI model, together with a variety of suggestions to overcome them. If the information contained herein does not assist you in overcoming your difficulties, please make contact with a PBI consultant, or the authors.

Notes

1 EMERGING EDUCATIONAL TECHNOLOGIES

1 See, for example, Ashdown, Carpenter, and Bovair (1991)
2 The extent to which teachers direct learning will depend upon their values and personal teaching styles. Some teachers prefer to set fairly definite guidelines, while others are prepared to negotiate processes and outcomes with their students.
3 The term 'intellectual disability' is synonymous with the terms 'mental retardation' or 'mental handicap' which are in common use in the United States and Great Britain respectively.

2 CLASSROOM DYNAMICS

1 In a totally child-centred context, such as early childhood education, 'skill-related material' might better be described as the substance of a learning experience.
2 For a discussion of cooperation in the classroom, see Johnson and Johnson (1987) and Johnson, Johnson, and Johnson-Holubec (1990) and Peer Tutoring (ERIC Research and Resource No. 30) (1991).

3 HUMAN LEARNING AND PROBLEM-SOLVING

1 Readers might find the following references of interest: Burton (1982), Kihlstrom (1987) and Klausmeier et al. (1979).
2 A short article by Denton (1988) may help clarify these ideas.
3 Costa (1991) has provided an extensive review of nearly 30 cognitive education programmes currently in use around the world.
4 For readers interested in other approaches, the following references may be useful: Deshler and Lenz (1989), Schumaker, Deshler, and Ellis (1986), Peat, Mulcahy, and Darko-Yeboah (1989); Feuerstein, Rand, and Hoffman (1979), Feuerstein, Rand, Hoffman, and Miller (1980).
5 See Paris, Lipson, and Wixson (1983).
6 See Manzo (1968), Palincsar and Brown (1983).
7 See, for example, Friedman, Scholnick, and Cocking (1990).
8 A similar notion was discussed by Tharp and Gallimore (1985). They suggested that 'knowing how' (to perform an act) is a logical prerequisite of 'knowing that' (rules and propositions apply and govern an activity).

4 AN OVERVIEW OF THE PBI MODEL

1 Several approaches to this problem may be familiar to you. Ausubel, for example, emphasized information networks (stressing the structure of the knowledge base

and the importance of prerequisite knowledge) while Bruner argued that knowledge is acquired through doing (which he called enactive learning), visualization (iconic learning), and through recognizing relationship (symbolic learning) – strategies which many teachers might use on a daily basis.

2 Some teachers may choose to begin PBI by developing a general plan, for example, an organizational plan for preparing homework.

3 This is the approach we recommend when the teacher and students are not fully familiar with plan development, use or adaptation.

4 There are, of course, recipe books which provide only the ingredients – without quantities or methods – that are used by experienced chefs. Saulnier's (1976) *La répertoire de la cuisine* is one example.

5 Hammond (1990) has used similar descriptions in his work on case-based planning which is based on the idea that new plans should be based on the planner's knowledge of past successes and failures. When a plan is unsuccessful in achieving the desired goal, it is a consequence of the planner's inadequate or incomplete knowledge of the situation or circumstances, rather than of poor planning skills.

6 If plans are written in a form which is incomprehensible to them, it is highly unlikely that it will be used. The important point is that students must USE the plan and, hence, we are not overly concerned here whether or not students use correct grammatical forms and structures.

7 You will recall from Chapter 3 that programmes like Verbal Self-Instruction Training and Strategies Programme for Effective Learning/Thinking prescribe the strategies and the method which students are to adopt. In PBI, the teacher provides a model and cultivates student analysis and evaluation of it.

5 PREPARING TO USE PBI

1 Peer tutoring is a relatively common procedure used in the primary grades – less common in the secondary school – which aims to develop positive learning and social interaction practices between students. Perhaps the most important principles guiding peer tutoring are that able students can present information accurately and in a form that other students can readily understand. For an overview of this area, the reader is directed to Foot, Morgan, and Shute (1990).

2 This is not meant to imply that children's spontaneity and their creative expression should be stifled – there is a vast difference between developing classroom practices which help the classroom function in an orderly way, and eliminating improvisation and imagination.

3 See Brown and Palincsar (1982) for details of reciprocal teaching.

4 The reader will recall from Chapter 3 that some teaching method, or 'treatments', may work well for some students and not for others because students have different skills, abilities and attitudes to learning (aptitudes).

6 STARTING PBI IN THE CLASSROOM

1 In this book we have not provided an expansive description of how to design or implement any particular peer tutoring or cooperative learning group work approach. For some practical ideas, the reader might locate the following references: Foot, Morgan, and Shute (1990), Johnson and Johnson (1987), and Johnson, Johnson, and Johnson-Holubec (1990).

8 PLANS IN THE SOCIAL AND AFFECTIVE DOMAINS

1 For an extensive overview of the area of behaviour disorders, see Conway (1990)

2 The use of specific coloured card for each step of the plan was not explained to M, as it was to be used in follow-up lessons in which the importance of each component was to be emphasized.

9 APPLICATIONS OF PBI FOR SCHOOL PERSONNEL

1 In Australia, the Early Literacy Inservice Course (ELIC) has adopted this approach very successfully.

10 TROUBLE-SHOOTING IN PBI

1 There are a number of writers who have catalogued the ideal characteristics of teachers. Readers interested in this area might consult the following: Association of Teachers Educators (1988), Dill (1990), Turney (1981) and Turney, Ellis, Towler, and Wright (1986).

References

Alberto, P.A., and Troutman, A.C. (1990). *Applied behavior analysis in the classroom* (3rd edn). Columbus: Merrill Publishing.

Ashdown, R., Carpenter, B., and Bovair, K. (eds) (1991). *The curriculum challenge: Access to the National Curriculum for pupils with learning difficulties*. London: Falmer Press.

Ashman, A.F., and Conway, R.N.F. (1989). *Cognitive strategies for special education*. London: Routledge.

Ashman, A.F., van Kraayenoord, C., and Elkins, J. (1992). Observations of students with learning difficulties in Grade 2 classrooms. Unpublished document, Fred and Eleanor Schonell Special Education Research Centre, The University of Queensland, St Lucia.

Association of Teacher Educators (1988). *Teacher assessment*. Reston, VA: Author.

Ausubel, D.P. (1963). *The psychology of meaningful and verbal learning*. New York: Grune and Stratton.

Beatty, W. and Troster, A. (1987). Gender differences in geographical knowledge. *Sex Roles*, 16, 565–90.

Berger, R.M., Guilford, J.P., and Christensen, P.R. (1957). A factor-analytic study of planning abilities. *Psychological Monographs*, 71, Whole No. 435.

Bransford, J., Sherwood, R., Vye, N., and Rieser, J. (1986). Teaching thinking and problem solving. *American Psychologist*, 41, 1078–89.

Brown, A.L., and Barclay, C.R. (1976). The effects of training specific mnemonics on the metamnemonic efficiency of retarded children. *Child Development*, 47, 71–80.

Brown, A.L., Bransford, J.D., Ferrara, R.A., and Campione, J.C. (1983). Learning, remembering and understanding. In P. Mussen (ed.), *Handbook of child psychology: Cognitive development* (Vol. 3) (pp. 77–166). New York: John Wiley.

Brown, A.L., and Campione, J.C. (1986). Psychological theory and the study of learning disabilities. *American Psychologist*, 14, 1059–68.

Brown, A.L., and Palincsar, A.S. (1982). *Inducing strategic learning from texts by means of informed, self-control training* (Tech. Rep. No. 262). Champaign, Ill.: University of Illinois at Urbana-Champaign, Center for the Study of Reading.

Bruner, J.S. (1966). *Toward a theory of instruction*. Cambridge, MA: Harvard University Press.

Burns, R.B., and Lash, A.A. (1986). A comparison of activity structures during basic skills and problem-solving instruction in seventh-grade mathematics. *American Educational Research Journal*, 23, 393–414.

Burton, A. (ed.) (1982). *The pathology and psychology of cognition*. London: Methuen.

Byrne, R.W. (1979). The form and use of knowledge in a decor-design task. Unpublished manuscript, University of St Andrews, Scotland.

Byrne, R.W. (1981). Mental cookery: An illustration of fact retrieval from plans. *Quarterly Journal of Experimental Psychology*, 33A, 31–7.

Campione, J.C., and Brown, A.L. (1978). Towards a theory of intelligence: Contributions from research with retarded children. *Intelligence*, 2, 279–304.

Canfield, J., and Wells, H.C. (1976). *100 ways to enhance self concept in the classroom: A handbook for teachers and parents*. Englewood Cliffs, NJ: Prentice-Hall.

Cantor, J.H., and Spiker, C.C. (1979). The effects of interactions on hypothesis testing in kindergarten and first-grade children. *Child Development*, 50, 1110–20.

Case, R. (1992, February). Fostering the development of central conceptual structures in the primary and middle school years. Paper presented at the Third International Conference of the International Association on Cognitive Education, Riverside, California.

Chapman, J.W., Silva, P.A. and Williams, S. (1984). Academic self-concept: A study of academic and emotional correlates in nine-year-old children. *British Journal of Educational Psychology*, 54, 284–92.

Conway, R.N.F. (1990). Behaviour Disorders. In A.F. Ashman and J. Elkins (eds) *Educating children with special needs* (pp. 148–86). Sydney: Prentice-Hall.

Conway, R.N.F. and Ashman, A.F. (1992). Training students with a mild intellectual disability to use metacognitive strategies in a special class context. Unpublished document, Special Education Centre, the University of Newcastle, NSW Australia.

Conway, R.N.F., Schofield, N.J., and Tierney, J. (1990). The Fair Discipline Code Project: A review of the application of the Fair Discipline Code in NSW secondary schools. Newcastle, NSW Australia: The University of Newcastle.

Costa, A.L. (1991). *Developing minds: A resource book for teaching thinking* (Rev. edn.) (Vols. 1 and 2). Alexandra, VA: Association for Supervision and Curriculum Development.

Cronbach, L.J., and Snow, R. E. (1977). *Aptitude and instructional methods*. New York: John Wiley.

Daniels, H. (1990). The modified curriculum: Help with the same or something completely different. In P. Evans and F. Varma (eds), *Special education: Past, present and future* (pp. 77–101). London: Falmer Press.

De Lisi, R. (1990). A cognitive-developmental model of planning. In S.L. Friedman, E.K. Scholnick, and R.R. Cocking (eds) *Blueprints for thinking: The role of planning in cognitive development* (pp. 79–109). Cambridge: Cambridge University Press.

Denton, L. (1988). Memory: not place, but process. *APA Monitor*, 19 (11), 4.

Derry, S.J., Hawkes, L.W., and Tsai, C. (1987). A theory of remediating problem-solving skills of older children and adults. *Educational Psychologist*, 22, 55–87.

Deshler, D.D., and Lenz, (1989). The Strategies Instructional Approach. *International Journal of Disability, Development and Education*, 36, 203–24.

Dill, D.D. (1990). *What teachers need to know: The knowledge, skills and values essential to good teaching*. San Francisco: Jossey-Bass.

Dinkmeyer, D., and Dinkmeyer, D. (Jr) (1981). *Developing understanding of self and others – D–1* (DUSO). New York: AGS.

Dixon, P. (1987) The structure of mental plans for following directions. *Journal of Experimental Psychology: Learning, Memory, and Cognition*, 13, 18–26.

Doyle, W. (1983). Academic work. *Review of Educational Research*, 53, 159–99.

Dreikurs, R., Grunwald, B., and Pepper, F. (1982). *Maintaining sanity in the classroom* (2nd edn). New York: Harper and Row.

Ellis, E.S. (1986). The role of motivation and pedagogy on the generalization of cognitive strategy training. *Journal of Learning Disabilities*, 19, 66–70.

ERIC Clearinghouse on Handicapped and Gifted Children (1991). Peer tutoring: When working together is better than working alone. *Research and Resource on Special Education*, 30.

Fennema, E., and Myer, M. (1989). Gender, equity, and mathematics. In W. Secada (ed.) *Equity in education*. New York: Falmer.

Ferguson, E.D. (1976). *Motivation: An experimental approach*. New York: Holt, Rinehart & Winston.

Feuerstein, R., Rand, Y., and Hoffman, M. (1979). *The dynamic assessment of retarded performers: The learning potential assessment device, theory, instruments, and techniques*. Baltimore, MD: University Park Press.

Feuerstein, R., Rand, Y., Hoffman, M., and Miller, R. (1980). *Instrumental Enrichment: An intervention for cognitive modifiability*. Baltimore: University Park Press.

Fields, B.A. (1991). Support for integration: Questioning the efficacy of the Resource/Remedial model of service delivery to academically handicapped children. In A.F. Ashman (ed.) *Currrent themes in integration* (Exceptional Children Monograph No. 2) (pp. 61–73). St Lucia: Fred and Eleanor Schonell Special Education Research Centre.

Foot, H.C., Morgan, M.J., and Shute, R.H. (eds) (1990). *Children helping children*. Chichester: John Wiley.

Fraser, B.J. (1986). Classroom environment. London: Croom Helm.

Fredericksen, N. (1984). Implications of cognitive theory for instruction in problem solving. *Review of Educational Research*, 54, 363–407.

Friedman, S.L., Scholnick, E.K., and Cocking, R.R. (eds) (1990). *Blueprints for thinking: The role of planning in cognitive development* (pp. 79–109). Cambridge: Cambridge University Press.

Gallagher, H. (1991). Teaching a Year 5 learning disabled student to use Process-Based Instruction plans to solve specific maths problems. Unpublished document, Fred and Eleanor Schonell Special Education Research Centre, The University of Queensland, Australia.

Galvin, P. (1989). Behaviour problems and cognitive processes. In D. Sugden (ed.). *Cognitive approaches to special education* (pp. 178–214). London: Falmer.

Gerber, M.M. (1983). Learning disabilities and cognitive strategies: A case for training or constraining problem solving? *Journal of Learning Disabilities*, 16, 255–60.

Glasser, W. (1985). *Control theory in the classroom*. New York: Perennial Library.

Hammond, K.J. (1990). Case-based planning: a framework for planning from experience. *Cognitive science*, 14, 385–443.

Harlow, J.M. (1848) Passage of an iron rod through the head. *New England Journal of Medicine*, 39, 389–393.

Haynes, M.C. and Jenkins, J.R. (1986) Reading instruction in special education resource rooms. *American Educational Research Journal*, 23, 161–190.

Hilgard, E.R. and Bower, G.H. (1966). *Theories of learning* (3rd edn). New York: Appleton-Century-Crofts.

Iran-Nejad, A. (1990). Active and dynamic self-regulation of learning processes. *Review of Educational Research*, 60, 573–602.

Johnson, D.W., and Johnson, R. (1987) *Learning together and alone: Cooperation, competition, and individualistic learning* (2nd edn). Englewood Cliffs, NJ: Prentice Hall.

Johnson, D.W., Johnson, R.T., and Johnson-Holubec, E. (1990). *Cirlces of learning: Cooperation in the classroom* (3rd edn). Edina, MN: Interaction Book Co.

Kihlstrom, J.F. (1987). The cognitive unconscious. *Science*, 237, 1445–52.

Klausmeier, H.J. and Associates. (1979). *Cognitive learning and development: Information-processing and Piagetian perspective.* Cambridge, Mass: Ballinger.

Kreitler, S., and Kreitler, H. (1986). Individuality in planning: Meaning patterns of planning styles. *International Journal of Psychology*, 21, 565–87.

Ladd, G.W. (1981). Effectiveness of a social learning method for enhancing children's social interaction and peer acceptance. *Child Development*, 52, 171–8.

Lockheed, M. (1985). Sex and social influence: A meta-analysis guided by theory. In J. Berger and M. Zelditch (eds) *Status, rewards, and influence* (pp. 406–27). San Francisco: Jossey-Bass.

Luria, A.R. (1973). *The working brain.* Harmondsworth: Penguin.

Luria, A.R. (1980). *Higher cortical functions in man* (2nd edn). New York: Basic Books.

Manzo, A.V. (1968). Improvement of reading comprehension through reciprocal questioning. Unpublished doctoral dissertation, Syracuse University, New York.

Marfo, K., and Mulcahy, R. (1991). Teaching cognitive strategies in the classroom: A content-based instructional model. In R. Mulcahy, J. Andrews, and R. Short (eds) *Enhancing learning and thinking.* New York: Praeger.

Marsh, G.E., Price, B.J., and Smith, T.E.C. (1983). *Teaching mildly handicapped children: Methods and materials.* St Louis: C.V. Mosby.

Means, B., and Knapp, M.S. (1991). Cognitive approaches to teaching advanced skills to educationally disadvantaged students. *Phi Delta Kappan*, 73, 282–9.

Meichenbaum, D., and Asarnow, J. (1978). Cognitive-behavioral modification and metacognitive development: Implications for the classroom. In P. Kendall and S. Hollon (eds), *Cognitive-behavioral interventions: Theory, research and procedure* (pp. 11–36). New York: Academic Press.

Meichenbaum, D.H., and Goodman, J. (1971). Training impulsive children to talk to themselves. *Journal of Abnormal Psychology*, 77, 115–26.

Miller, G.A., Galanter, E.H., and Pribram, K.H. (1960). *Plans and the structure of behavior.* New York: Holt, Rinehart & Winston.

Moely, B., Hart, S., Santulli, K., Leal, L., Johnson, I., Rao, N., and Burney, L. (1986). How do teachers teach memory skills? *Educational Psychologist*, 21, 55–71.

Morsink, C.V., Soar, R.S., Soar, R.M., and Thomas, R. (1986). Research on teaching: Opening the door to special education classrooms. *Exceptional Children*, 53, 32–40.

Palincsar, A.S., and Brown, A.L. (1983). *Reciprocal teaching of comprehension-monitoring activities* (Tech. Rep. No. 269). Champaign, Ill.: University of Illinois at Urbana-Champaign, Center for the Study of Reading.

Paris, S.G., Lipson, M.Y., and Wixson, K.K. (1983). Becoming a strategic reader. *Contemporary Educational Psychology*, 8, 293–316.

Paris, S.G., Saarnio, D.A., and Cross, D.R. (1986). A metacognitive curriculum to promote children's reading and learning. *Australian Journal of Psychology*, 38, 107–23.

Peat, D., Mulcahy, R.F. and Darko-Yeboah, J. (1989). SPELT (Strategies Program for Effective Learning/Thinking): a description and analysis of instructional procedures. *Instructional Science*, 18, 95–118.

Petersen, L., and Gannoni, A.F. (1989). *Stop, think, do: Training social skills while maintaining student behaviour.* Melbourne: ACER.

Pressley, M., Levin, J.R., and Bryant, S.L. (1983). Memory strategy instruction during adolescence: When is explicit instruction needed? In M. Pressley and J.R. Levin (eds) *Cognitive strategy research: Psychological foundations* (pp. 25–49). New York: Springer-Verlag.

Rogoff, B., and Gardner, W. (1984). *Everyday cognition: Its development in social contact*. Cambridge, Mass.: Harvard University Press.

Saulnier, L. (1976). *Le répertoire de la cuisine*. Woodbury, NY: Barron's Educational Series.

Savell, J.M., Twohig, P.T., and Rachford, D.L. (1986). Empirical status of Feuerstein's 'Instrumental Enrichment' (FIE) technique as a method of teaching thinking skills. *Review of Educational Research*, 56, 381–409.

Schumaker, J.B., Denton, P.H., and Deshler, D.D. (1984). *Learning Strategies Curriculum: The paraphrasing strategy*. Lawrence, KS: University of Kansas.

Schumaker, J.B., Deshler, D.D., and Ellis, E.S. (1986). Intervention issues related to the education of LD adolescents. In J.K. Torgesen and B.Y.L. Wong (eds), *Psychological and educational perspectives on learning disabilities* (pp. 329–65). Orlando, FL: Academic Press.

Schumaker, J.B., and Sheldon, J. (1985). *The sentence writing strategy – Instructors' manual*. Lawrence, KS: University of Kansas.

Shuell, T.J. (1986). Cognitive conceptions of learning. *Review of Educational Research*, 56, 411–36.

Strain, P.S., Odom, S.L., and McConnell, S. (1984). Promoting social reciprocity of exceptional children: Identification, target behavior selection, and intervention. *Remedial and Special Education*, 5, 21–8.

Tharp, R.G., and Gallimore, R. (1988). *Rousing minds to life: Teaching, learning and schooling in social context*. Cambridge: Cambridge University Press.

Turney, C. (ed.) (1981). *Anatomy of teaching*. Sydney: Novak.

Turney, C., Ellis, K.J., Towler, J., and Wright, R. (1986). *The teacher's world of work*. Sydney: Sydmac Academic Press.

Turnure, J.E. (1986). Instruction and cognitive development: Coordinating communication and cues. In M.J. Shepard and L. Gelzheiser (eds), *Exceptional Children, Special Issue, Competence and instruction: Contributions from cognitive psychology*, 53, 109–17.

Webb, N. (1984). Stability of small group interaction and achievement over time. *Journal of Educational Psychology*, 76, 211–24.

Webb, N. (1985). Student interaction and learning in small groups. In R. Slavin, S. Sharan, S. Kagan, R. Hertz-Lazarowitz, N. Webb, and R. Schmuck (eds) *Learning to cooperate, cooperating to learn* (pp. 147–172). New York: Plenum Press.

Wellman, H.M. (1990). *The child's theory of mind*. Cambridge, MA: Bradford.

Wheldall, K. (1991a). *Discipline in schools: Psychological perspective and the Elton Report*. London: Routledge.

Wheldall, K. (1991b). Managing troublesome classroom behaviour in regular schools: A positive teaching perspective. *International Journal of Disability, Development and Education*, 38, 99–116.

Wolman, B.B. (1973). *Dictionary of behavioral science*. New York: Van Nostrand.

Wong, B.Y.L. (1986). A cognitive approach to teaching spelling. *Exceptional Children*, 53, 169–73.

Wragg, J. (1989). *Talk sense to yourself*. Melbourne: ACER.

Ysseldyke, J.E., Thurlow, M.L., Christenson, S.L., and Weiss, J. (1987). Time allocated to instruction of mentally retarded, learning disabled, emotionally disturbed, and nonhandicapped elementary students. *Journal of Special Education*, 21, 43–55.

Appendix

Use the following pages as a master copy for plan-making practice.

You can also use the master copy to develop prototype plans as you begin to use plans in your classroom.

MAKING A PBI PLAN

(Refer to Box 5.8 on p. 90, which provides a checklist for making a PBI plan)

1 What is the goal?

2 What do the students know?

3 What should the students know after using the plan?

A short PBI plan checklist
1 Is the plan a sequence which will allow the student to progress unassisted from one step to the next?
2 Can the person complete the plan unassisted?
3 Does the plan require thoughts and actions, not simply provide a set of directions?
4 Does the plan contain steps that can be˙ identified as cuing, acting, monitoring or verifying steps (or a combination of these components)?

Initial draft

(Draft your plan on this page and use the following page to set out your final version.)

Final Version

Index